RAF FIGHTERS
VS
LUFTWAFFE BOMBERS

Battle of Britain

ANDY SAUNDERS

OSPREY PUBLISHING
Bloomsbury Publishing Plc
PO Box 883, Oxford, OX1 9PL, UK
1385 Broadway, 5th Floor, New York, NY 10018, USA
E-mail: info@ospreypublishing.com
www.ospreypublishing.com

OSPREY is a trademark of Osprey Publishing Ltd

First published in Great Britain in 2020

A catalogue record for this book is available from the British Library.
Missing photo
ISBN: PB: 9781472808523; eBook 9781472808547; ePDF 9781472808530;
XML 9781472821744
20 21 22 23 24 10 9 8 7 6 5 4 3 2 1

Edited by Tony Holmes
All artwork by Jim Laurier
Maps and diagrams by www.bounford.com
Index by Alan Rutter
Typeset by PDQ Digital Media Solutions, Bungay, UK
Printed and bound in India by Replika Press Private Ltd

Osprey Publishing supports the Woodland Trust, the UK's leading woodland
conservation charity.

To find out more about our authors and books visit
www.ospreypublishing.com. Here you will find extracts, author interviews,
details of forthcoming events and the option to sign up for our newsletter.

Hurricane I attacking He 111H cover art

On 30 August 1940, during the height of the Battle of Britain, eight
Hurricanes from No. 79 Sqn took off from RAF Biggin Hill at 1115 hrs.
When the fighters intercepted a mixed formation of He 111s, Bf 109s and
Bf 110s over Dorking, Surrey, South African pilot Flg Off E. J. 'Teddy'
Morris, flying as 'Blue 1', led his section in a head-on attack against a
formation of around 18 Heinkel bombers. Morris initially dived down on the
formation before pulling up to attack them head-on at 16,000ft. However, as
he flew in amongst the He 111s, he misjudged the distance of the second 'vic'
behind the leading aircraft and collided with one of the bombers. Morris felt a
thump on his right wing, immediately after which the Hurricane spun away
violently and he was forced to bail out. The Heinkel, having lost a wing,
plummeted to earth at Newdigate, Surrey, where it exploded upon hitting the
ground. Three of the crew were killed and two captured, one of them seriously
injured. Morris duly claimed one He 111 destroyed by collision. (Artwork by
Jim Laurier)

Defiant I attacking Do 17Z cover art

On 26 August 1940, a small number of Do 17Zs from 7./KG 3 departed their
base at St Trond, Belgium, to attack RAF airfield targets in southern England.
As the formation approached the Kent coastline, escorted by a Bf 109 fighter
screen from I./JG 3, Hurricanes of No. 56 Sqn, Spitfires of Nos. 610 and 616
Sqns and Defiants of No. 264 Sqn were scrambled to intercept them. It was
the Defiants' task to target the bombers, and several crews from that squadron
subsequently made claims, including Sgt Edward Thorn and his gunner,
Sgt Fred Barker, who were credited with two Do 17s and a Bf 109 destroyed.
In total, No. 264 Sqn claimed six Dornier victories and one damaged,
although only three Do 17Zs were lost in the English Channel and another
crash-landed in France. One of those downed over the water landed on the
Goodwin Sands at low tide – two of its crew were captured and two were
dead. This Do 17Z, Wk-Nr. 1160 5K+AR, is claimed to be the aircraft
recovered from the sea by the RAF Museum in 2013. (Artwork by
Jim Laurier)

Previous Page

Evidence of what sustained hits from batteries of 0.303-in. machine guns
could do can be seen in the fuselage of this Do 17Z of 8./KG 77, shot down
on 3 July 1940 at Paddock Wood, Kent, after multiple determined attacks
from three Hurricanes of No. 32 Sqn. (Author's Collection)

CONTENTS

INTRODUCTION

The iconic scenario of RAF fighter squadrons sweeping in to attack massed formations of German bombers on the call of 'Tally Ho!' is very much an image that comes to mind when one thinks of the Battle of France and the Battle of Britain. To an extent, that is how it was. However, those battles were preceded by much smaller actions, with sections or flights from RAF fighter squadrons engaging solitary raiders along the length of Britain's east coast during late 1939 and early 1940. At this early stage in the conflict, much was being learned by attackers and defenders alike in brief thrust-and-parry skirmishes. These early engagements were, more often-than-not, very one-sided affairs that often saw bullet-riddled Heinkel He 111s ending their days wrecked along the east and northeast coastline or shot down into the cold waters of the North Sea.

However, the large-scale clashes that would follow later in 1940 were far removed from these early skirmishes, although the bombers brought down over England and Scotland in the opening months of the war certainly bore scars that told just how deadly sustained attacks from batteries of eight Browning 0.303-in. machine guns could be. It was, though, just the beginning. What was happening on either side of the English Channel in the early months of 1940 would shape the Luftwaffe bomber force's tactics and RAF Fighter Command's response.

Whilst the German bomber arm had already begun to suffer badly at the

The first enemy aircraft brought down on British soil was this He 111 of KG 26, which force-landed at Humbie, Scotland, on 28 October 1939 after being attacked by Spitfires of Nos. 602 and 603 Sqns. (Author's Collection)

hands of RAF Fighter Command following the commencement of *Blitzkreig* operations on 10 May 1940, it was certainly the case, thus far, that neither side had properly assessed the other's strengths and weaknesses in combat. This included proper consideration by Luftwaffe commanders as to how best to protect bomber formations and, conversely, for the RAF to work out the most effective tactics to employ when engaging them.

Over France and the Low Countries, the massed Luftwaffe bomber formations were mostly engaged by Allied fighters that were almost chancing upon the

A crew member inspects 0.303-in. bullet holes in the fuselage of a He 111 from KG 26 that managed to struggle back to base. The unit took part in Luftwaffe air operations in the west, including in Norway and during the Battle of Britain. (Author's Collection)

enemy by luck rather than by any form of judgement or control. In fact, no integrated command and control structure existed within the French air defence system under which the RAF was then operating. When German aircraft were engaged, it was generally the result of patrolling fighters finding the enemy, rather than being controlled onto them. Consequently, it needed the defenders to be in the right place at the right time in order to find and engage enemy bombers. RAF Fighter Command could not put standing patrols constantly in the air to cover all the likely targets. This was also the situation it subsequently faced when covering the evacuation from Dunkirk, where there was no effective radar coverage and no ground-based command and control system. Patrolling RAF fighters had just to hope the enemy would be encountered whilst they were operating over the evacuation area. Thus, a degree of anticipation as to where the Luftwaffe might next attack was required. For all of that, though, RAF fighters quickly began to take a toll on the German bomber force. Lessons of attack and defence were being learned by both sides.

Notwithstanding the rout of the Allies in France during the spring of 1940, RAF Fighter Command had given a very good account of itself in terms of victories claimed – squadrons had, however, suffered an exceedingly high attrition rate. Nevertheless, the Luftwaffe recorded a total loss of some 1,814 aircraft (of all types) on the Western Front from 3 September 1939 up until the Allied withdrawal from France at the end of June. A high percentage of the combat losses in this grand total had been the result of RAF fighter action, which, for this period, had almost exclusively involved Hurricanes. For the same period, the RAF had lost 1,067 aircraft (of all types). At the very least, these balance sheets give us, to a limited extent, an indication of the successes achieved by RAF fighters against a numerically superior enemy.

As the Luftwaffe established itself on the French and Belgian coasts and faced the British Isles, so it became possible for the Germans to mount massed and escorted bombing raids against mainland and coastal targets. Of course, the aircraft undertaking the early operations across the North Sea in late 1939 and early 1940 did not have the luxury of fighter escorts. Now, at least for targets in the area of London and southeast England, Bf 109 and Bf 110 fighters were able to give cover.

Four of No. 264 Sqn's Defiants tuck in close during a training sortie from Kirton-in-Lindsey, Lincolnshire, in July 1940. The lead aircraft is N1535/PS-A in which Sqn Ldr Philip Hunter led the squadron into action in the Battle of Britain during late August. He was ultimately lost in this machine whilst chasing a Ju 88 over the Channel on the 24th of the month. To the right of N1535 is L7026/PS-V, which Plt Off Eric Barwell used to shoot down a Bf 109 on the same day Hunter was killed. (Tony Holmes Collection)

Nevertheless, the Luftwaffe learned the lesson that all major air forces learned during World War II – massed daylight raids, even if escorted, were risky undertakings. Thus, as losses rose against what were limited successes, so the Luftwaffe's bombing tactics changed towards the end of 1940 as the *Kampfgeschwaderen* reverted to predominantly nocturnal raids. With no effective RAF nightfighter force yet in place, and the limited effectiveness of anti-aircraft guns, it was the safest option for the attackers.

In terms of the aircraft types ranged against each other, the Luftwaffe employed three main medium bombers – the Junkers Ju 88, Heinkel He 111 and Dornier Do 17. The bomb load each could carry was roughly comparable at around 1,500kg for the Ju 88, 2,000kg for the He 111 and 1,000kg for the Do 17. Similarly, each carried a defensive armament of flexibly mounted MG 15 machine guns of 7.92mm calibre (usually around five weapons per aircraft, although this could vary with individual field modifications). Additionally, the Luftwaffe bomber fleet's order of battle included the formidable Junkers Ju 87 Stuka. A veritable flying artillery piece, the dive-bomber could carrying a bomb load of up to 1,800kg, but had only three 7.92mm machine guns with which to defend itself – two fixed, forward firing, and one flexible, rearward firing.

Overall, the defensive firepower on the various bombers seems woefully inadequate against the weapons ranged against them from defending Spitfires, Hurricanes and Defiants. In the case of the former two types, this was eight 0.303-in. machine guns per fighter, while the Defiant had a battery of four such weapons in a powered turret.

In this book I will examine the actions of the Luftwaffe's bomber force, and all four of the main types it fielded, in 1940, as well as the three main defending RAF fighter types. The equipment used and the tactics and experiences of the men involved are all covered in this examination of what was then, up to that point in history, the largest aerial clash between two opposing air forces. What transpired during those actions in 1940 would provide both the Luftwaffe and the RAF (and other foreign air forces) with a steep and rapid learning curve that duly shaped tactics, equipment development, and bombing and defensive strategies for both sides. To a very large extent, the 'rule books' for aerial combat operations, both defensive and offensive, were figuratively torn up and new operating procedures developed to suit the reality of battle, rather than textbook theory.

CHRONOLOGY

1939

16 October   Spitfires of Nos. 602 and 603 Sqns engage and shoot down two Ju 88s of *Kampfgeschwader* (KG) 30 off the Scottish coast, these being the first successes achieved by RAF Fighter Command against Luftwaffe bombers attacking Britain.

28 October   First enemy aircraft brought down on the mainland British Isles near Humbie, Scotland, when a He 111 of *Stab.*/KG 26 is shot down – again by Spitfires of Nos. 602 and 603 Sqns.

29 November   In Directive No. 9, the *Führer*, Adolf Hitler, decrees, *inter alia*, that the Luftwaffe should attack the British mainland and coastal targets, including ports, depots, food and oil storage facilities, and embark upon the destruction of industrial plants.

1940

11 January   Spitfires of No. 66 Sqn attack a He 111 of I./KG 26 off Cromer, Norfolk. The aircraft is damaged and makes a forced landing in neutral Denmark, where the crew destroy the bomber. Return fire from the Heinkel demonstrates the defensive potential of the MG 15 by damaging two of the attacking Spitfires.

3 February   The first enemy aircraft to be brought down on English soil in World War II crashes near Whitby, Yorkshire, the He 111 of 4./KG 26 being shot down by a section of Hurricanes from No. 43 Sqn.

10 May   Germany launches its attack in the West – the *Blitzkreig* – thus bringing to an end the 'Phoney War' on the Western Front that saw relatively limited aerial activity and engagements between RAF Hurricanes based in France and lone Luftwaffe reconnaissance and bomber aircraft. While the Wehrmacht surges into France, Belgium and thence on to Luxembourg and the Netherlands, the Luftwaffe bomber force is committed *en masse* to support the German advance. RAF fighter squadrons become heavily engaged against them, pilots encountering large

Flt Lt Bob Boothby and Sgt 'Sammy' Allard of Hurricane-equipped No. 85 Sqn claimed 14 German bombers destroyed between 10 and 16 May 1940. (Tony Holmes Collection)

	formations of enemy bombers for the first time.
11 May	Hurricanes of Nos. 87 and 607 Sqns become the first RAF fighters to engage the Ju 87 Stuka, in the Tirlemont region of Belgium.
16 May	Air Chief Marshal H. C. T. Dowding, Commander-in-Chief RAF Fighter Command, sets out concerns about sending further fighters to France, pointing out that in the preceding few days the equivalent of ten squadrons have been sent there. He states that the further reinforcement of fighters will result in 'the final, complete and irremediable defeat of this country'.
17 May	The intense aerial fighting in France soon results in the first RAF fighter pilots achieving ace status with five or more victories. Among this elite band is Sgt Geoffrey 'Sammy' Allard, a Hurricane pilot with No. 85 Sqn. On this date he downs no fewer than three He 111 bombers.
26 May	No. 46 Sqn, with its Hurricanes, along with Gladiator-equipped No. 263 Sqn arrive in Norway.

No. 264 Sqn claimed considerable success over Dunkirk, although the totality of those victory claims do not stand close scrutiny. Later, during the Battle of Britain, the type did not prove to be a success and losses were high. Here, an aircraft from the unit is examined after it had sustained serious damage over Dunkirk in late May 1940. (Author's Collection)

29 May	The so-called 'Glory Day' of the Defiant, with crews from No. 264 Sqn *claiming* 37 enemy aircraft destroyed in two actions above Dunkirk. This figure is now known to represent significant over-claiming.
30 May–4 June	Evacuation of British and Allied forces from Dunkirk during Operation *Dynamo*. Heavy aerial fighting between aircraft from RAF Fighter Command and German bombers, and their fighter escorts, targeting the operation.
3 June	Evacuation of British forces from Narvik, Norway, begins.
8 June	Aircraft carrier HMS *Glorious* returning from Norway with Nos. 46 and 263 Sqns embarked is sunk in the North Sea by the Kriegsmarine with the loss of all aircraft and the majority of RAF personnel.
19–20 June	Overnight, He 111s of KG 4 attack targets in East Anglia, losing five aircraft to nightfighter Blenheims and, surprisingly, Spitfires of Nos. 19 and 74 Sqns operating nocturnally. This is the largest attack against Britain to date, involving 70 bombers.
23 June	From the German viewpoint, the all-out Luftwaffe air assault on Britain (*Lufschlacht am England*) commences on this day.
4 July	Attacks by Ju 87 units on the Royal Navy dockyard at Portland, Dorset, and on a convoy in the English Channel are the first bombing sorties carried out against Britain involving a fighter escort. In the event, no RAF opposition is met.

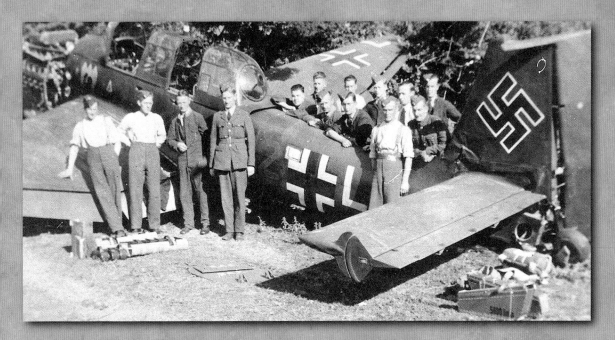

This Ju 87 of 4./StG ?? was shot down at St Lawrence, on the Isle of Wight, on 8 August 1940 during an attack against the shipping of Convoy CW9 *Peewit*. The dive-bomber had fallen victim to the Hurricane of No. 145 Sqn flown by Plt Off Peter Parrott. Although the pilot of the Stuka, Unteroffizier Fritz Pittroff was captured, his gunner, Unteroffizier Rudolf Schubert, had been killed in the engagement. (Author's Collection)

10 July	Officially, for the Air Ministry, this is the first day of the Battle of Britain. It is marked by RAF Fighter Command engagements with Luftwaffe bombers, principally the Do 17s of KG 2.
10 July–7 August	A period characterised by intermittent light raids and skirmishing along the south coast and English Channel, including attacks on coastal convoys that are frequently engaged by RAF fighters.
8 August	Originally designated the first day of the Battle of Britain by the Air Ministry, the 8th sees repeated dive-bombing attacks by Ju 87s on Convoy CW9 *Peewit*. Across three main raids this day, RAF fighters engage the Stukas and their escorts.
12 August	Significant daylight bombing by the Luftwaffe against British targets, including airfields and Chain Home (CH) and Chain Home Low (CHL) radar sites. Raids intercepted by RAF fighters, who achieve good results against the bomber force.
13 August	The Luftwaffe launches Eagle Day (*Adler Tag*), an all-out assault to destroy the RAF in the air and on the ground. RAF fighters intercept the largest formations of German bombers encountered thus far, with the Luftwaffe losing 44 aircraft and having a further 36 damaged to varying degrees.
15 August	Another hard-fought day, with Luftwaffe bombing attacks ranging from the northeast to the southwest of England. The intercepted raids endure heavy punishment as RAF Fighter Command effectively deals with

German bombers – 75 Luftwaffe aircraft are lost on operations and 15 damaged.

16 August
An escorted raid by He 111s of KG 55 on the Great West Aerodrome (Heathrow) and an attack by Ju 87s of *Stukageschwader* (StG) 2 on RAF Tangmere, West Sussex, are both effectively engaged by RAF Fighter Command. Evidence of punishment caused by eight 0.303-in. machine guns is clearly seen on a He 111 that crash-landed near Worthing, West Sussex.

18 August
The hardest fought day of the Battle of Britain sees massed attacks by escorted Luftwaffe bomber formations. RAF fighters are heavily engaged against high- and low-level raids, resulting in 71 Luftwaffe aircraft being lost and 25 damaged in engagements with Spitfires and Hurricanes.

22 August
Defiant-equipped No. 264 Sqn, 'rested' at RAF Kirton-in-Lindsey, Lincolnshire, after losses over Dunkirk, returns south to RAF Hornchurch, Essex.

24–26 August
No. 264 Sqn is badly mauled in battle by Bf 109s, losing seven aircraft and having four more damaged in two days of action. In total, nine aircrew are listed as killed or missing in action.

28 August
No. 264 Sqn is again withdrawn to RAF Kirton-in-Lindsey.

30 August
A large, escorted raid of He 111s from KG 53 fights its way inland to attack Radlett aerodrome, Hertfordshire, being intercepted by Spitfires from Nos. 222 Sqn and Hurricanes of Nos. 56, 151, 242 and 601 Sqns during the course of the mission.

7 September
The 'Blitz' begins as the Luftwaffe changes its tactics from bombing airfields to attacking London. Massed daylight raids again attract fierce opposition from RAF Fighter Command.

7–8 September
Attacks on London continue, with the near-continual night bombardment commencing on this date and lasting until 11 May 1941. Nocturnal attacks mean the German bombers are very largely immune from fighter interception.

15 September
Often marked as the climax of the battle, the day sees massed escorted bomber formations attacking London fiercely engaged by RAF fighters, which enjoy considerable success.

27 September
The last heavily fighter-escorted bombing raids on the British Isles are undertaken on this day. The Luftwaffe's *modus operandi* is changing, and the RAF's defensive strategy evolves accordingly.

7 October
One of the last large-scale fighter-escorted daylight bomber attacks of the campaign, on the

The He 111 crews of KG 26 had long flights over the North Sea from their bases in Norway to contend with, as well as the prospect of meeting RAF fighters off the northeast coast of Britain as they approached their targets. (Author's Collection)

Westland factory in Yeovil, Somerset, meets heavy opposition. Two bombers (from a force of 25 Ju 88s) and seven fighters (from the 50-strong Bf 110 escort) are lost.

15 October   By now, Luftwaffe mass-escorted daylight bomber attacks are unusual, having been all but abandoned in favour of daylight Bf 109E 'Jabo' fighter-bomber attacks and mass night-time bomber raids. This day sees significant fighter-bomber attacks on London.

29 October   The tactic of fast fighter-bomber attacks continues, although this day also sees the very last fighter-escorted daylight bombing raid against mainland Britain with an attack on Portsmouth, Hampshire, by 12 Ju 88s escorted by a large force of Bf 109s.

31 October   Although the last 'official' day of the Battle of Britain, RAF fighters have very largely only been called upon to intercept singleton Luftwaffe bombers operating over the mainland since late September. During the period 10 July to 31 October 1940, RAF Fighter Command has learned a great deal in terms of what tactics and methodology are the most effective to employ against the Luftwaffe bomber force.

11 November   Despite the cessation of Luftwaffe daylight attacks on Britain, the Italian *Regia Aeronautica* carries out a mass fighter-escorted daylight bombing attack against the east coast. Intercepted by RAF Fighter Command, the Italians suffer significant losses.

The attack is a failure and is not repeated. Very clearly, RAF fighters have by now become the masters of the skies over the British Isles during daylight hours.

19–20 November   Daylight fighting against Luftwaffe bombers over Britain is by now very much a thing of the past, except against the occasional singleton raider. With the bombing force now attacking by night, RAF Fighter Command's nascent nightfighter force is struggling to cope, and enjoys few successes. However, there is a turning point on the night of 19–20 November when future high-scoring ace Flt Lt John Cunningham of No. 604 Sqn uses an Airborne Interception (AI) radar-equipped Bristol Beaufighter IF to down a Ju 88 – the first aircraft to be brought down over land using AI radar.

29–30 December   This night sees one of the heaviest nocturnal raids on London. Ironically, the night 'Blitz' is an indirect consequence of the success of RAF fighters against escorted (and unescorted) daylight bombing raids. The Luftwaffe experience no losses on this night, and only one RAF nightfighter is seen – it is noted that 'this failed to attack'.

31 December   By the end of 1940, RAF Fighter Command has achieved clear ascendancy over the daylight bomber and experienced radical changes. By 31 December it can deploy 71 squadrons and 1,467 fighters in an expanded Command consisting of six groups following the addition of Nos. 9 and 14 Groups.

DESIGN AND DEVELOPMENT

HURRICANE I

In 1934, the Air Ministry issued Specification F.7/30 in response to demands from the RAF for new generation fighter aircraft. Earlier, in 1933, Hawker's aircraft designer, Sydney Camm, had conducted discussions with the Directorate of Technical Development about a monoplane based on the existing Hawker Fury biplane fighter. This had quickly led to the drafting of the specification, which included Camm's preference for the armament to be installed in the wings instead of the aircraft's nose.

Hawker's initial submission for a F.7/30 proposal, the P.V.3, was essentially a scaled-up version of the Fury and it was not selected as a government-sponsored prototype. After the P.V.3's rejection, Camm commenced work on a new design involving a cantilever monoplane arrangement complete with a fixed undercarriage, armed with four machine guns and powered by the 600hp, evaporatively cooled, Rolls-Royce Goshawk engine. The original 1934 armament specification for what would evolve into the Hurricane was for a similar armament fitment to the Gloster Gladiator – four machine guns, with two in the wings and two in the fuselage that were synchronised to fire through the propeller arc.

By January 1934, the proposal's detailed drawings had been finished, but these failed to impress the Air Ministry enough for a prototype to be ordered. Camm's response was to further develop the design, incorporating a retractable undercarriage and replacing the unsatisfactory Goshawk engine with a new Rolls-Royce design,

HURRICANE I WING GUNS

The Hurricane I was fitted with four Browning 0.303in. machine guns in each wing. It usually took a two-man team nine minutes to rearm (refuel and re-oxygen) a Hurricane I, each Browning being loaded with 332 rounds of ammunition, which, at 20 rounds per second, would last just 17 seconds. Being grouped together in a single bay in each wing, and accessible from above, the magazines of the Hurricane I could be replenished more quickly than those of the Spitfire (it took 23 minutes to turn the latter around). Although the Brownings were very reliable, they were regularly criticised by RAF pilots for not providing them with sufficient punch when it came to shooting down German fighters and bombers.

initially designated the PV-12, which went on to become the Merlin engine. In September 1934 Camm again approached the Air Ministry, and the response this time was favourable, resulting in a prototype of the 'Interceptor Monoplane' being ordered.

Prototype Hurricane K5083 performed its maiden flight on 6 November 1935. Essentially, it was still a development of the Fury airframe, with both types being built around an internal 'skeleton' of four wire-braced alloy and steel tube longerons – this structure was renowned for its simplicity of construction, durability and capacity for absorbing punishment. The Hurricane also benefited from Hawker's long-standing partnership with Rolls-Royce, whose newly developed Merlin I engine proved to be the ideal powerplant. Finally, the fighter boasted no fewer than four Browning 0.303-in. machine guns in each wing.

The Hurricane went into production for the Air Ministry in June 1936, and it finally entered squadron service on 25 December 1937 with No. 111 Sqn. The issuing of the aircraft to frontline units saw the RAF make the jump from the era of biplanes to monoplane fighters.

The aircraft's manufacture had been eased by using conventional construction methods that also meant squadrons could perform many major repairs without external support from Hawker. Recognising the value of the Hurricane, the Air Ministry rapidly procured the fighter in large numbers prior to the outbreak of World War II. Indeed, by September 1939 the RAF already had 18 Hurricane-equipped squadrons in service.

During early 1940 the Hurricane I evolved from being fitted with the Merlin II, powering a fixed-pitch, two-bladed, wooden Watts propeller, to utilising the Merlin III paired with a three-bladed de Havilland (metal) or Rotol (wooden) constant-speed propeller. Further refinements included the fitting of armour plating behind the pilot's seat and upgrading the wings from being fabric covered to an all-metal construction.

SPITFIRE I

In 1931, the Air Ministry issued the requirement for a modern fighter capable of a level flying speed of 250mph, and Supermarine's aircraft designer, R. J. Mitchell, responded with the Type 224 to fill this role. An open-cockpit monoplane with bulky gull-wings and a large, fixed, undercarriage, and powered by the Goshawk engine, the aircraft made its first flight in February 1934 but was rejected in favour of the more conventional Gladiator biplane.

Mitchell and his design team immediately embarked on a series of cleaned-up designs, using their experience with the Schneider Trophy-winning seaplanes as a starting point and leading to the Type 300, with a retractable undercarriage and reduced wingspan. This design was submitted to the Air Ministry in July 1934, but again was not accepted. It then went through a series of changes, including the incorporation of a faired, enclosed cockpit, oxygen-breathing apparatus, smaller and thinner wings, and the newly developed, more powerful PV-12 engine. In November 1934, Mitchell, with the backing of Supermarine's owners,

A Hurricane I of No. 1 Sqn is refuelled at RAF Tangmere just prior to the outbreak of war. It is fitted with an early two-bladed wooden fixed-pitch Watts propeller. The battery of guns (four in each wing) can be clearly seen. (Author's Collection)

Three Spitfire Is of No. 65 Sqn sit at readiness at RAF Northolt, west London, in early 1940. The aircraft lack the outer yellow ring to their fuselage roundels and fin stripes, both of which were introduced from June 1940. K9907/YT-D and K9911/YT-E were downed by Bf 109s on 8 July and 8 August respectively, while L1094/YT-H was damaged in the same action that saw the destruction of YT-E. (Author's Collection)

SPITFIRE I/II WING GUNS

The Spitfire I and IIA were armed with four Browning 0.303-in. machine guns in each wing, this weapons fit being given the A-type wing designation with the advent of cannon-armed Spitfire IBs. Rate of fire was 20 rounds per second per gun (160 rounds per second overall), and each cartridge fired ball, armour-piercing, tracer or incendiary bullets weighing 11.3 grams at 2,430ft per second. Total weight of projectiles fired was four pounds per second. Ammunition capacity (300 rounds per gun) was enough for 16 seconds of continuous firing in the Spitfire.

Vickers-Armstrong, started detailed design work on the refined version of the Type 300.

On 1 December 1934, the Air Ministry issued contract AM 361140/34, providing £10,000 for the construction of Mitchell's improved Type 300 design, and on 3 January 1935 it formalised the contract with a new specification, F.10/35, written around the aircraft. In April 1935, the armament was changed from two Vickers 0.303-in. machines guns in each wing to four Browning 0.303-in. machine guns.

On 5 March 1936, the prototype, K5054, took off on its first flight with Capt Joseph 'Mutt' Summers, chief test pilot for Vickers, at the controls. He is quoted as saying 'Don't touch anything' on landing after an eight-minute flight. The Spitfire's maiden flight took place four months after its contemporary, the Hawker Hurricane, had first flown.

Test flying soon revealed the Spitfire to be a very good aircraft, although it was not perfect. The rudder was oversensitive and its top speed was just 330mph, which was only a little faster than Sydney Camm's new Hurricane. In mid-May, however, Summers flew K5054 to RAF Martlesham Heath, Suffolk, and handed it over to the Aeroplane and Armament Experimental Establishment for service testing. A few weeks later, on 3 June 1936, the Air Ministry placed an order for 310 Spitfires, although the first production Spitfire, K9787, did not roll off the Woolston, Southampton, assembly line until mid-1938. A further order was placed for another 200 Spitfires on 24 March that same year. Eventually, the Spitfire entered operational service with No. 19 Sqn at Duxford on 4 August 1938.

Defiant I N1535 was delivered to No. 264 Sqn at Kirton-in-Lindsey in July 1940, where it became the personal aircraft of the unit CO, Sqn Ldr Philip Hunter, and carried the individual code letter 'A' that was usually reserved for the commanding officer. The aircraft also carried the squadron leader's pennant on either side of the fuselage under the cockpit. Although he had stepped down as CO on 19 August 1940, Hunter insisted on staying on for a few extra days to properly hand over to his replacement. Hunter was shot down in N1535 on 24 August 1940 while pursuing a Ju 88 out to sea. No trace of the aircraft, Hunter or his gunner, Plt Off Harry King, were ever found.

No. 264 Sqn's Defiant I L7013/PS-U leads a tight formation in late July 1940 during a training sortie from Kirton-in-Lindsey. This aircraft was damaged by Bf 109s on 24 August, whilst L7025/PS-Z was shot down by a German fighter over Herne Bay, Kent, two days later. (Tony Holmes Collection)

DEFIANT I

In April 1935, the Air Ministry issued Specification F.9/35, calling for a high-speed two-seat day and nightfighter with armament concentrated in a power-operated turret. Twelve companies responded, including Boulton Paul of Norwich, which submitted its P.82 proposal. In April 1937, the Air Ministry accepted the P.82 design straight off the drawing board, ordering 87 of the type.

Fitted with a Rolls-Royce Merlin III engine, and now named Defiant, Boulton Paul's prototype, P8310, made its first flight in the hands of Cecil Feather on 11 August 1937. It was found to be an excellent flying machine without any serious vices. Importantly for a gun platform, it was also exceptionally stable, with its concentrated battery of four Browning 0.303-in. machine guns being mounted in a power-operated turret behind the pilot.

The Defiant's all-important turret made it unusual for a single-engined fighter, the aircraft being conceived very much as a 'bomber formation destroyer'. Whilst conventional wisdom might have us believe that this was a hopelessly outmoded design concept for modern air fighting, it was certainly not as ill-conceived as has subsequently been noted by numerous historians. Such suggestions inevitably arose from its poor performance during the daylight fighting in the Battle of Britain, where it proved to be no match for enemy fighters.

Certainly, the Defiant lacked forward-firing guns, and had to be brought into a fighting position by its pilot for the gunner to get a bead on his quarry. However, it was never designed for fighter-versus-fighter combat – notwithstanding the fact that, during trials against a No. 65 Sqn Spitfire in 1940, the Defiant 'scored' time and again in a turning dogfight and the Spitfire not once. These, though, were artificially contrived tests for a fighter-versus-fighter scenario, and it must be borne in mind that RAF calculations in the 1930s were wholly based upon the premise that any bomber attacks against Britain would be flown from Germany without protection from escorting fighters. Thus, when designed, the Defiant did not need to fear fighter interference, and the concept of it as a bomber formation destroyer was theoretically sound. Reality, of course, soon overtook theory during the summer of 1940.

In general terms, the Defiant employed conventional all-metal construction methods, but one of its unusual features was the attachment of the light alloy skins of wings and fuselages to stringers and ribs, which were then fixed to the wing spars and fuselage frames, thus avoiding any need to pre-form the skins. Moreover, by

DEFIANT I

35ft 4in.

12ft 2in.

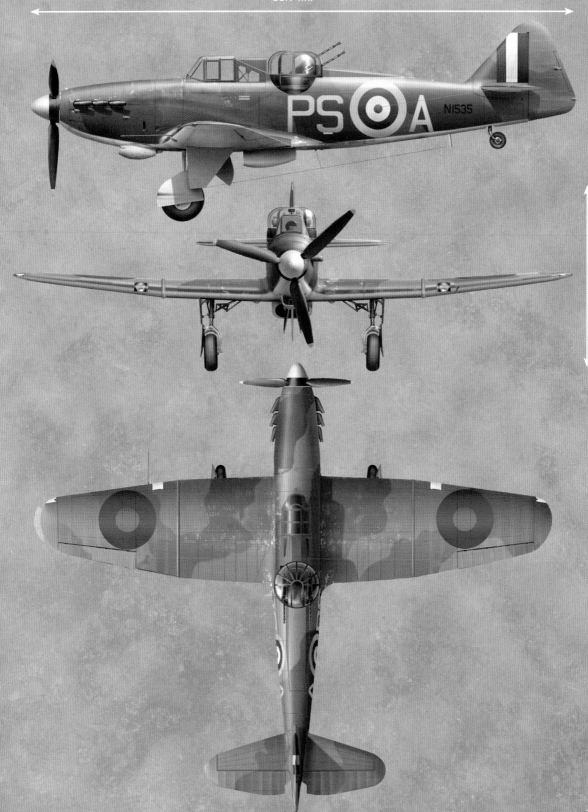

39ft 4in.

BOULTON PAUL TYPE A Mk II TURRET

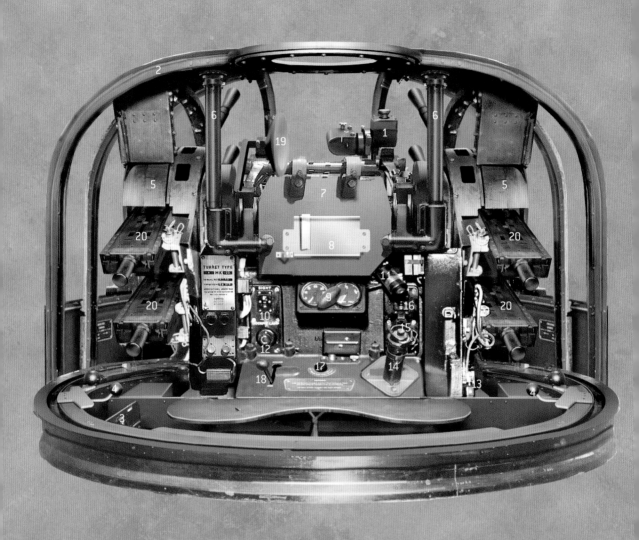

1. Gunsight	8. Writing pad holder	15. Gun firing button
2. Turret cupola	9. Oxygen regulator panel	16. Fairing lever
3. Turret control panel	10. Gunsight on/off switch	17. Turret high-speed switch
4. Turret rotation locks (x2)	11. Panel lamp	18. Turret free and engaged lever
5. Gun cradles (x2)	12. Panel lamp on/off switch	19. Adjustable cheek rest
6. Cupola supports (x2)	13. Intercom plug	20. 0.303-in. Browning machine guns (x4)
7. Armour plating	14. Gun control column	

riveting the skins whilst flat, this method of construction provided an exceptionally 'clean' surface finish.

The first production Defiant (L6950) was fitted with light bomb racks as per the Air Ministry specification, although these were absent from later production models and never used in service. With a wing span of 39ft 4in., a length of 35ft 4in., a height of 11ft 4in. and an all-up weight of 8,318lb, the Defiant was a deceptively large aeroplane – but then it had to accommodate the Boulton Paul Type A Mk II turret, which weighed 590lb, plus its gunner.

By the time war broke out, only three production Defiants had been delivered. However, by January 1940, more than 40 were in service, and orders stood at 135. The first unit to equip with the type was No. 264 Sqn in December 1939.

In service, the tactical and strategic situation for which the Defiant had been conceived had evaporated. Now, in the summer of 1940, Bf 109 and Bf 110 fighters were within range of southern Britain, and bomber formations attacking the mainland were, for the most part, heavily escorted. Thus, if the Defiant was to perform as a bomber formation destroyer then it had to either penetrate a defensive fighter screen or deal with the Messerschmitts when they pounced. All the time, of course, the gunner was reliant on his pilot getting the aircraft into the best attacking or defensive position.

There can be no doubt that without fighter interference the Defiant would have been a good asset for use against bomber streams. The intended tactic was that a section of three or more aircraft would move into a position to one side of and below the enemy formation where defensive fire was at its weakest or non-existent. The theory was simply that the only way for an engaged bomber to avoid a torrent of fire from the Defiants was for the target aircraft to break out of formation, thus rendering itself vulnerable to attack from conventional fighters. Theory and practice, of course, were two different things, and the presence of escorting fighters blew a hole in this optimistic plan. However, had the Germans failed to overrun France and the Low Countries, then the Defiant would likely have proved a formidable opponent against unescorted bomber formations threatening the British mainland.

BOULTON PAUL TYPE A Mk II TURRET

The Type A Mk II turret was hydraulically powered via its own electrical pump, and had two speeds of movement that could rotate it through 360 degrees. The four 0.303-in. Browning machine guns could not depress below 17 degrees above the horizontal when trained forward so as to avoid the gunner accidently hitting the aircraft's propeller. Owing to the limits posed by the gunsight, the maximum elevation that a gunner of normal size could achieve was about 72 degrees, or up to 85 degrees with a small gunner in the turret. Electrical cut-outs prevented rounds fired by the guns from hitting any part of the airframe. In total, the turret carried 2,400 rounds of ammunition – 600 bullets per gun, stored in tanks beneath each pair of 0.303s. Expended at a rate of 20 rounds per second, this gave the turret around 30 seconds of firing time in total. Unlike the guns of the Spitfire and Hurricane, fired cases and links were retained on-board the Defiant and not ejected.

Ju 87B STUKA

Two sub-types of the Junkers dive-bomber were operational during the period covering the Battles of France and Britain, namely the B-1 and B-2. However, the origins of the Ju 87 in use during 1940 went back much further to the quite different looking Junkers K 47, which was developed as early as 1929.

The second version of the Ju 87 to go into production, the 'Berta' would become the main production version of the aircraft during the early part of World War II. Fitted with a Junkers Jumo 211A engine developing 1,200hp for take-off, the 'Berta' was a considerable improvement over the Ju 87A – its cockpit was streamlined, and 'spats' replaced the 'Anton's' mainwheel 'trousers'. One area that remained the same, however, was its forward-firing armament, which consisted of a single 7.92mm machine gun in each wing. The additional engine power enabled the 'Berta' to carry both a two-man crew *and* a 500kg bomb – the rear gunner/radio operator had to remain on the ground when the Ju 87A was fully loaded due to its Junkers Jumo 210D producing just 600hp. The Ju 87B was also fitted with additional racks under the wings to carry four 50kg bombs.

In October 1938, five early-production Ju 87Bs were sent to the *Condor Legion* in Spain, where they operated with considerable success during the closing months of the civil war in that country.

During 1937–38, a total of 395 Ju 87As and Bs were built, including prototypes and pre-production aircraft. In 1938, production of the dive-bomber was transferred to the Weser plant at Berlin-Templehof, the first aircraft coming off the new production line that autumn. During 1939, a total of 557 'Bertas' came off the line at Templehof, and on the outbreak of war with Poland on 1 September 1939, these aircraft equipped nine *Stukagruppen*.

During the closing months of that year, the B-2 succeeded the B-1 on the production line. The new version featured minor changes, including ejector exhaust stubs, hydraulically powered cooling gills for the engine and an improved propeller with broader wooden blades (the B-1 had a metal-bladed propeller). The B-2 could potentially carry a maximum bomb load of 1,000kg.

The Ju 87 Stuka dive-bomber had been used with devastating effect during the campaigns in Poland, Norway, France and the Low Countries. However, it did not fare well against RAF fighters during the Battle of Britain, and losses were high. These unarmed B-2s from 5./StG 2 'Immelmann' are seen returning from a mission en masse. After approaching their target in attack formation, Stukas generally headed for home in fairly loose groups, as seen here. (Author's Collection)

Developed in parallel with the B-2, the Ju 87R was intended for extended range operations. Also built in reasonably large numbers, this variant was fitted with an additional 150-litre fuel tank in each outer wing section and could carry a 300-litre drop tank on the single bomb rack under each wing. The extra tankage gave the R-model a maximum range of 1,400km – twice that of the Ju 87B.

Do 17Z

In 1932, the *Heereswaffenamt* (Ordnance Department) issued a specification for a 'freight aircraft for the German State Railway' and a 'high-speed mail aeroplane for *Deutsche Lufthansa*'. Both descriptions, of course, were to hide the true nature of the design, which was in contravention of the Treaty of Versailles. The Dornier factory at Friedrichshafen began work on the aircraft on 1 August that same year.

The *Reichsluftfahrtministerium* (RLM – German Ministry of Aviation) designated the new aircraft Do 17, and on 17 March 1933 the go-ahead for the building of prototypes was given. At the end of 1933, the RLM issued an order for a 'high-speed aircraft with a twin tail' and for a 'freight aircraft with special equipment' – in other words, a bomber. The original design (Do 17 V1) configuration of 1932 saw the aircraft sporting a single vertical stabiliser, and Dornier continued developing that model. The Do 17 was first demonstrated in mock-up form in April 1933, with the 'special equipment' to be fitted later so as to disguise the aircraft's offensive role.

In April 1934, the Dornier works at Manzell began project 'definition', with the Do 17's defensive armament being designed and issues with the bomb release mechanism being ironed out. Production of these prototypes began on 20 May 1934, and the type first flew six months later on 23 November. The twin-tailed V2 (powered by low-compression BMW VI 6.3 engines) undertook its maiden flight on 18 May 1935 and was evaluated, together with the V1, by the RLM in June. During trials, the V1 proved to be only marginally stable, resulting in it being retrofitted with a twin tail. However, the aircraft was destroyed in a crash after an engine failure on 21 December 1935.

The V3, also fitted with a twin tail, was originally planned to be powered by Hispano-Suiza engines, but as these were unavailable it had BMW VI 7.3 engines (like the V1) installed instead – the aircraft flew for the first time on 19 September 1935. The V1 prototype, therefore, remained the only Do 17 built with a single stabiliser. Dornier was then ordered to produce the V4 prototype. The tests of the 'twin-tailed' V4, V6 and V7 prototypes were positive, and yet more prototypes like the V8 emerged as the forerunner of the long-range reconnaissance version, while the V9 was tested as a high-speed airliner.

The initial production variants were the Do 17E-1 bomber, which was tested with two Daimler-Benz DB 600 engines, and the Do 17F-1 reconnaissance aircraft, powered like the early prototypes by BMW VI engines, which entered production in late 1936. The first Luftwaffe units converted to the Do 17 in early 1937, and the type in use during the Battle of Britain was predominantly the Do 17Z as a bomber and, in smaller numbers, the Do 17P in the reconnaissance role. Both variants used Bramo-Fafnir 323 engines.

Ju 88

In August 1935, the RLM submitted its requirements for an unarmed, three-seat, high-speed bomber with a payload of 800–1,000kg. Amongst the manufacturers to submit a design in response to this requirement was Junkers with its Ju 88 – the company actually developed two parallel designs, the Ju 85 and the Ju 88. The twin-engined Ju 85, requested by the RLM, differed from the Ju 88 in its use of a twin fin tail unit. Despite official backing, the aircraft was never put into production.

Junkers then reverted to its initial single-finned Ju 88 design in June 1936, and it was given clearance by the RLM to build two prototypes – the V1 and V2. The aircraft was to have a range of 2,000km and be powered by two engines. Three further prototypes were to be built, all of which were powered by Jumo 211 engines. The Ju 88 V3, V4 and V5 differed from the earlier prototypes by being equipped with three defensive armament positions in the rear cockpit. They were also able to carry two 1,000kg bombs, one under each inner wing panel.

The aircraft's first flight was made by the prototype Ju 88 V1, which bore the civil registration D-AQEN, on 21 December 1936. It initially achieved speeds of up to 580km/h, which delighted the Commander-in-Chief of the Luftwaffe, Generalfeldmarschall Hermann Göring. Here was an aircraft that could finally fulfil the promise of the high-speed *Schnellbomber* ('fast bomber') – a light bomber that, in theory at least, would be so fast that it could outrun defending fighters of the period. The fifth prototype set a 1,000km closed-circuit record in March 1939, the V5 carrying a 2,000kg payload at an astonishing speed of 517km/h.

Almost 18 months earlier, in October 1937, Generalluftzeugmeister Ernst Udet (who was the Luftwaffe's director of research and development) had also ordered the development of the Ju 88 as a heavy dive-bomber. By 1938, radical modifications to the airframe had produced just such an aircraft. Its wings were strengthened and dive brakes added, the fuselage was extended and the crew increased to four. As a dive-bomber, the Ju 88 was capable of pinpoint deliveries of heavy loads. However, despite modifications, dive-bombing still proved too stressful for the airframe, and later in the war tactics were changed so that bombs were delivered from a shallower (45-degree) diving angle. Aircraft and bombsights were modified accordingly, and dive brakes removed. With an advanced Stuvi dive-bombing sight, accuracy was excellent.

Production was badly delayed by developmental problems, and although the Ju 88 was planned for service introduction in 1938, it

The *Lotfernrohr 7* (*Lot* meant 'Vertical' and *Fernrohr* meant 'Telescope') bombsight installed in the nose section of the ventral gondola, and the four external bomb carriers – to which ordnance has been attached – inboard of the engines, are clearly visible in this view of an early-production Ju 88A-1. (Tony Holmes Collection)

eventually reached frontline squadrons on the very day Poland was invaded by Germany. Manufacturing rates remained painfully slow, with Junkers only managing to build one Ju 88 per week due to persistent technical problems.

Despite the Ju 88's much-vaunted dive-bombing capability, the aircraft was used almost exclusively as a level bomber throughout 1940.

He 111

Following its defeat in World War I, Germany was banned from operating military aircraft by the Treaty of Versailles. However, the nation's re-armament had started in earnest in the 1930s, and this was initially kept secret because it violated the treaty. The early development of military bombers was, therefore, disguised as a programme for the building of civilian transport aircraft.

Among the designers seeking to benefit from German re-armament was Ernst Heinkel, who decided to create the world's fastest passenger aircraft – an objective which was met with scepticism by Germany's aircraft industry and its political leadership.

In June 1933 Albert Kesselring visited Heinkel's headquarters in his role as head of the Luftwaffe's Administration Office. At that point, Germany had only the *Luftfahrtkommissariat* (aviation commissariat), rather than a State Aviation Ministry. Kesselring was hoping to build a new air force out of the Flying Corps being constructed in the Reichswehr, and for this he required modern aircraft. He duly convinced Heinkel to move his factory from Warnemünde to Rostock and to adopt mass production techniques, the company soon employing 3,000 workers.

Features of the He 111 were apparent in the He 70 Blitz mail aeroplane/faster passenger transport, the first example of which came off the production line in 1932. The single-engined aircraft immediately started breaking records, with a standard four-passenger version attaining a speed of 380km/h when powered by a 600hp BMW VI engine. The He 70 was designed with elliptical wings, which became a feature of this and many subsequent Heinkel designs, and drew the interest of the Luftwaffe – the latter was looking for an aircraft with both bomber and transport capabilities. Heinkel subsequently spent some 200,000 man hours designing the He 111, which was in effect a twin-engined version of the Blitz. The new aircraft preserved the He 70's elliptical inverted gull wing and small, rounded control surfaces, and was powered by two BMW VI engines.

The prototype He 111 flew for the first time on 24 February 1935, with chief test pilot Gerhard Nitschke being ordered not to land back at the company's factory airfield at Rostock-Marienehe due to its runway being deemed to be too small for such a large aircraft. Instructed to head for the central *Erprobungstelle* Rechlin test facility instead, Nitschke ignored these orders and successfully landed back at Rostock-Marienehe. Once on the ground he stated that the He 111 handled perfectly well at slower speeds, which meant there was no danger of overshooting the runway.

Nitschke also praised the prototype's high speed, very good flight and landing characteristics, stability during cruising and descent, single-engine flight

performance, and the total absence of nose-drop when the undercarriage was extended. During the second test flight, however, he discovered there was insufficient longitudinal stability when using full power to climb and maintain horizontal flight – Nitschke had to use an excessively high amount of force to operate the aileron controls.

By the end of 1935, three prototypes had been produced, these aircraft being given the civilian registrations D-ALIX, D-ALES and D-AHAO. D-ALES duly became the first prototype of the He 111A-1 on 10 January 1936, and it later received recognition as the 'fastest passenger aircraft in the world' when it recorded a speed exceeding 402km/h.

The first He 111B made its maiden flight in the autumn of 1936, with the first production examples being rolled out from the Heinkel factory at Rostock

A He 111P delivers its payload of bombs during the Battle of Britain. The type was one of the mainstays of the assault on Britain in 1940–41 and first saw Luftwaffe service during the Spanish Civil War. (Author's Collection)

later that same year. Seven B-0 pre-production aircraft were built, these being powered by Daimler-Benz DB 600C engines fitted with variable-pitch propellers. The B-0 could also carry 1,500kg of ordnance in a vertical bomb cell, while the B-1 had minor improvements such as the installation of a revolving gun mount in the nose and a flexible Ikaria turret beneath the fuselage. The RLM ordered 300 He 111B-1s, with the first being delivered to the Luftwaffe in January 1937. The first operational use of the He 111 came just two months later in Spain when the *Condor Legion* used four B-1s to target Republican-held airfields in support of Nationalist forces during Battle of Guadalajara.

1. Pilot's seat
2. Propeller pitch indicator
3. Flaps position indicator
4. Flaps control lever
5. Landing gear indicator
6. Cockpit lights (x2)
7. Pitot heating switch
8. Cockpit illumination control
9. Throttle levers
10. Throttle lever friction damper
11. Propeller pitch control levers
12. Magneto switches
13. Landing gear lever
14. Oil cooler controls
15. Elevator pitch control wheel
16. Clock
17. Rudder pedals
18. Control column and yoke
19. Artificial horizon
20. Autopilot course indicator
21. Autopilot light
22. Turn and bank indicator
23. Vertical speed indicator
24. Blind landing system indicator
25. Altimeter
26. Repeater compass
27. Directional gyro and autopilot direction indicator
28. Turn and slip indicator
29. Tachometers (x2)
30. Supercharger pressure gauges (x2)
31. Water temperature gauges (x2)
32. Oil temperature gauges (x2)
33. Fuel pressure indicator
34. Oil pressure indicator
35. Observer's oxygen mask
36. MG 15 machine gun, saddle drum and fired cases holder
37. Spare MG 15 saddle drum magazine
38. MG 15 tool and spares kit
39. Observer's fold-down seat
40. Map and chart holder
41. Rudder trim controls
42. Observer's cushion for bomb aiming and firing MG 15
43. Course indicator
44. Radiator cooler controls (x2)
45. Escape hatch handle
46. Oxygen regulator
47. Airspeed indicator
48. Crew intercom switches

TECHNICAL SPECIFICATIONS

Hurricane I production underway at Hawker's Kingston-upon-Thames factory just prior to the outbreak of war. (Author's Collection)

HURRICANE

Toting eight 0.303-in. machine guns and capable of speeds in excess of 300mph, the Hurricane I was the world's most advanced fighter when issued to the RAF in December 1937. Although technically eclipsed by the Spitfire come the summer of 1940, Hurricanes nevertheless outnumbered the former type during the Battle of Britain by three-to-one, and downed more Luftwaffe aircraft than the Vickers-Supermarine fighter. Indeed, it is estimated that Hurricane pilots were responsible for four-fifths of all enemy aircraft destroyed in the period July to October 1940, with squadrons claiming 1,593 victories. This averaged out to 44.25 kills per unit, compared with more than 60 kills for squadrons equipped with Spitfires. Having taken over-claiming into account, the leading Hurricane unit with substantiated kills was No. 303 'Polish' Sqn, with 51.5 victories (although it actually claimed 121), followed by No. 501 Sqn with 40.25 victories (it claimed 101). The latter unit also holds the record for the highest number of days engaged – 35 – of any Fighter Command squadron during the Battle of Britain. Conversely, No. 501 Sqn also suffered more losses than any of its contemporaries, having an astonishing 41 Hurricanes destroyed.

Hurricane I Specification	
Type:	single-engined monoplane fighter
Crew:	pilot
Dimensions:	
Length:	31ft 5in. (9.58m)
Wingspan:	40ft 0in. (12.19m)
Height:	13ft 0in. (3.96m)
Weights:	
Empty:	4,982lb (2,260kg)
Max T/O:	7,490lb (3,397kg)
Performance:	
Max Speed:	324mph (521km/h)
Range:	600 miles (965km)
Powerplant:	Rolls-Royce Merlin II/III
Output:	1,030hp (768kW)
Armament:	
Eight Browning 0.303-in. machine guns in wings	
Production:	
4,200 Mk Is	

SPITFIRE I/II

The only British fighter to remain in production throughout World War II, the exploits of the Spitfire are legendary. More than 20,000 were produced in mark numbers ranging from I through to 24. This total also included more than 1,000 built as dedicated Seafire fleet fighters for the Royal Navy. Spitfire Is and IIs served only briefly in frontline squadrons with the RAF once the war had started, but their pilots were responsible for achieving impressive scores against the Luftwaffe in 1940. In the Battle of Britain, a total of 529 German aircraft were shot down by Spitfires serving with 20 units of Fighter Command. Conversely, 361 Spitfires were lost and 352 damaged during this same period. Finally, of the ten top-scoring squadrons in Fighter

A flight of No. 222 Sqn Spitfire Is takes off over a solitary, parked, Spitfire I of No. 610 Sqn that seems to have undergone repairs to what looks to have been some serious damage to its fuselage. Where and when this photograph was taken remains unknown, as No. 222 Sqn flew primarily from Hornchurch during the summer of 1940 and No. 610 Sqn was based at Biggin Hill, some 18 miles away. (Author's Collection)

Command, six of them were equipped with Spitfires. Although the early mark Spitfires were notorious for their light armament, short range and overheating engines (particularly during ground handling) due to inadequate cooling, many of the pilots who flew them regarded these first production machines as the best handling of the entire breed due to their excellent power-to-weight ratio and beautifully harmonised flying controls.

Spitfire IA Specification	
Type:	single-engined monoplane fighter
Crew:	pilot
Dimensions:	
Length:	29ft 11in. (9.12m)
Wingspan:	36ft 10in. (11.23m)
Height:	11ft 5in. (3.48m)
Weights:	
Empty:	4,810lb (2,182kg)
Loaded Weight:	5,844lb (2,651kg)
Performance:	
Max Speed:	355mph (571km/h)
Range:	575 miles (925km)
Powerplant:	Rolls-Royce Merlin II/III
Output:	1,030hp (768kW)
Armament:	
Eight Browning 0.303-in. machine guns	
Production:	
1,567 Mk IA/Bs and 921 Mk IIA/Bs	

DEFIANT I

Entering squadron service in December 1939, the Defiant initially proved to be very successful in its designated role of bomber destroyer, especially when deployed in mixed formations with single-seat fighters in support. The aeroplane was less effective against enemy fighters, except if attacked from above and behind. Otherwise, the Defiant proved to be an easy target for the Bf 109E, with 14 having been lost by No. 264 Sqn during Operation *Dynamo*. By the end of the Dunkirk evacuation

The cramped and somewhat dangerous Boulton Paul Type A Mk II turret of the Defiant I, with its battery of four 0.303-in. Browning machine guns. The turret, minus ammunition and the gunner, weighed 590lb. (Author's Collection)

No. 141 Sqn had also been formed with the Defiant. Flying from RAF West Malling, Kent, it served with No. 11 Group from 3 June until 21 July, when it was withdrawn after suffering heavy losses to Bf 109s in its first action on 15 July. Having made good its *Dynamo* losses, No. 264 Sqn only lasted six days in the frontline upon its return to RAF Hornchurch, in No. 11 Group, in late August 1940.

Defiant I Specification	
Type:	single-engined monoplane fighter
Crew:	pilot and turret gunner
Dimensions:	
Length:	35ft 4in. (10.77m)
Wingspan:	39ft 4in. (12.00m)
Height:	12ft 2in. (3.70m)
Weights:	
Empty:	6,078lb (2,757kg)
Max T/O:	8,318lb (3,773kg)
Performance:	
Max Speed:	304mph (489km/h)
Range:	465 miles (748km)
Powerplant:	Rolls-Royce Merlin III
Output:	1,030hp (768kW)
Armament:	
Four Browning 0.303-in. machine guns in dorsal turret	
Production:	
723 Mk Is	

Ju 87B STUKA

One of the most feared weapons of the early war years, the Junkers Ju 87 struck terror into the hearts of those unfortunate enough to be on the ground beneath it. Dubbed the Stuka (an abbreviation of *Stürzkampfflugzeug* – dive-bomber aircraft), the prototype had first flown in late 1935 powered by a Rolls-Royce Kestrel engine and with twin fins. By the time it entered series production two years later, the Ju 87B had a solitary fin, a Junkers Jumo 211 engine and large 'trousered' landing gear. It was every inch a dive-bomber, featuring a heavy bomb crutch that swung the weapon clear of the fuselage and propeller arc before it was released. Capable of diving at angles of up to 80 degrees, the aircraft could deliver more than 1,500lbs of ordnance with great accuracy. First blooded in Spain by the *Condor*

'Like a flock of huge birds', a *Staffel* of Ju 87Bs from StG 77 lifts off virtually as one from Caen during the early weeks of the Battle of Britain. Each aircraft is armed with a single SC 250 250kg bomb on the centreline and a SC 50 50kg bomb beneath either wing. (Tony Holmes Collection)

Ju 87B Specification	
Type:	single-engined monoplane dive-bomber
Crew:	pilot and rear gunner
Dimensions:	
Length:	36ft 5in. (11.10m)
Wingspan:	45ft 3.25in. (13.80m)
Height:	13ft 2in. (4.01m)
Weights:	
Empty:	5,980lb (2,713kg)
Max T/O:	9,369lb (4,250kg)
Performance:	
Max Speed:	211mph (339km/h)
Range:	490 miles (788km)
Powerplant:	Junkers Jumo 211Da
Output:	1,100hp (820kW)
Armament:	
Two fixed MG 17 7.92mm machine guns in wings and one MG 15 7.92mm machine gun on flexible mounting in rear cockpit; maximum bomb load of 1,102lb (500kg) on centreline and four 110lb (50kg) bombs under wings.	
Production:	
697 B-1s and 225 B-2s	

Legion in 1937, the Ju 87's finest hour came in support of the *Blitzkrieg* campaign waged by the Wehrmacht in Poland in September 1939 and across western Europe in May–June 1940. Although Ju 87s badly damaged seven airfields and three CH radar stations, and destroyed 49 aircraft during the early stages of the Battle of Britain, more often than not formations of Stukas would lose up to half their number or be forced to turn back before reaching their target after coming under sustained attack from Spitfire and Hurricane squadrons. Indeed, during just six days of combat from 12 to 18 August, 41 Ju 87s were destroyed.

Ju 88

One of the Luftwaffe's most important, and versatile, combat aircraft types, the Ju 88 was developed to answer a requirement for a high-speed medium bomber with a dive-bombing capability. An 'improved' Ju 88 came into service in August 1940, designated the A-5. It featured longer-span, strengthened wings with inset metal-skinned ailerons and a considerably increased bombload. Free of performance restrictions that had

Ju 88A-1 Specification	
Type:	twin-engined monoplane bomber
Accommodation:	pilot, navigator, bomb aimer/gunner and flight engineer/gunner
Dimensions:	
Length:	47ft 2in. (8.43m)
Wingspan:	65ft 10.50in. (20.08m)
Height:	15ft 11in. (4.85m)
Weights:	
Empty:	16,975lb (7,699kg)
Max T/O:	22,840lb (10,360kg)
Performance:	
Max Speed:	292mph (470km/h)
Range:	1,696 miles (2,730km)
Powerplant:	two Junkers Jumo 211Bs
Output:	2,400hp (1790kW)
Armament:	
Five or six MG 15 7.92mm machine guns in nose, rear cockpit and ventral gondola; maximum bomb load of 4,409lb (2,000kg) in bomb-bay and on underwing racks	
Production:	
1,885 Ju 88As were built in 1939–40	

Some of the 1,885 Ju 88As produced by Junkers in 1939–40 are assembled at the company's Bernburg factory. When, in the autumn of 1938, the RLM decided that the Ju 88 was to be the Luftwaffe's standard medium bomber, it instructed Junkers to aim for a maximum monthly production rate of 300 aircraft. The only way this could be achieved was for the manufacturer to distribute Ju 88 production amongst Germany's aircraft companies, with five 'groups' being responsible for various parts of the bomber. All sections were then transported to Bernburg for final assembly. (Tony Holmes Collection)

The navigator of this He 111H from II./KG 1 sits precariously on the open cockpit door hatch while giving the pilot directions as the latter taxis out at the start of a mission from Montdidier in the summer of 1940. The 'Cow riding a bomb' unit badge of 4./KG 1 can be seen on the fuselage immediately below the open hatch. Note also the *Lotfernrohr 7A* bombsight protruding from the lower nose glazing. (Tony Holmes Collection)

hamstrung the A-1, the new aircraft performed admirably in the summer and autumn of 1940 with the handful of units that received it. Thanks to its more modern design and better engines, subsequent versions of the aircraft such as the A-4, which was fitted with twice as many guns, still had sufficient performance available to avoid it being as vulnerable to enemy fighters as the He 111 and Do 17. The aircraft was almost aerobatic, and its speed gave the Ju 88 a better chance of outrunning British fighters than any other German bomber of the period. Continually upgraded and reworked during World War II, around 2,000 Ju 88 bombers were built per year between 1940–43.

He 111

The He 111 was the staple medium bomber of the Luftwaffe's *Kampfgeschwader* throughout World War II, and by the eve of the conflict, the redesigned H- and P-models had begun to enter service – the new variants had the distinctive fully glazed nose area and revised ventral gondola. When Germany invaded Poland on 1 September 1939, the Luftwaffe had 21 *gruppen* and one *staffel* equipped with the He 111 – a total of 789 aircraft. The bomber was, therefore, in the vanguard of operations during this campaign, as well as during the Phoney War in the West, the occupation of Norway in the spring of 1940 and the onslaught on the Low Countries. Indeed, by

the time of the *Blitzkrieg* in the West, *Luftflotten* 2 and 3 possessed a total of 1,120 twin-engined bombers, of which approximately half were He 111s. Carrying a heavier bombload than any of its contemporaries then in frontline service, the He 111P/H was also heavily utilised during the Battle of Britain and in the day and night Blitz on Britain.

He 111P-4 Specification	
Type:	twin-engined monoplane bomber
Accommodation:	pilot, navigator, bomb aimer, ventral and dorsal gunners
Dimensions:	
Length:	53ft 9.5in. (16.40m)
Wingspan:	74ft 1.75in. (22.60m)
Height:	13ft 1.5in. (4.00m)
Weights:	
Empty:	17,760lb (8,015kg)
Max T/O:	29,762lb (13,500kg)
Performance:	
Max Speed:	200mph (322km/h)
Range:	1,224 miles (1,970km)
Powerplant:	two Daimler-Benz DB 601A-1s
Output:	2,200hp (1,640kW)
Armament:	
Six or seven MG 15 7.92mm machine guns in nose, beam, dorsal, ventral and (optional) tail positions; maximum bomb load of 4,410lb (2,000kg) in bomb-bay	
Production:	
1,208 He 111H/Ps were built in 1939–40	

Do 17

The least numerous of the trio of medium bombers employed by the Luftwaffe during the Battle of Britain, the Do 17, like the He 111, was derived from a high-speed mailplane/airliner built to meet a *Deutsche Lufthansa* requirement from the early 1930s. Sometimes referred to as the *Fliegender Bleistift* ('flying pencil'), the aeroplane was converted into a *Schnellbomber*. The Do 17's layout had two engines mounted on a 'shoulder wing' structure, the aircraft also possessing a twin tail fin configuration. Entering frontline service with the Luftwaffe in early 1937, the Do 17 soon proved popular among its crews thanks to the aircraft's exceptional handling qualities,

especially at low altitude. This in turn made the Do 17 harder to hit than other German bombers. Indeed, Dornier units specialised in terrain-following raids because the aircraft's robust radial engines performed best at low altitude. Such attacks were made in an attempt to evade fighter opposition, crews relying on the bomber's exceptional manoeuvrability to get them out of trouble. In late 1938 Dornier switched production to the definitive Do 17Z variant. Driven by the need to provide the bomber with better underside protection and more crew space for maximum operational efficiency, the Z-model had an entirely redesigned forward fuselage. Although the most reliable of the Luftwaffe's bombers in the first year of World War II, the Do 17 lacked the load-carrying capability of the He 111 and the speed of the Ju 88, and production ceased in the early summer of 1940.

The pilot of a Do 17Z from Le Culot-based 9./KG 3 stares down from the cockpit of his spotless bomber while he waits for the rest of the four-man crew to board the aircraft through the open hatch in the underside of the aircraft. The Do 17Z carried five flexibly mounted 7.92mm MG 15 machine guns. These were drum fed, with each drum holding 75 rounds. Spare magazines were held on special brackets arranged near each gun position. The guns were each fitted in a flexible Ikaria ball-and-socket mounting that gave a wide arc of fire, although the rear cockpit weapons had restrictor rails fitted around them. The lower guns could be fired through an angle of 40 degrees either side. (Author's Collection)

Do 17Z-2 Specification	
Type:	twin-engined monoplane bomber
Accommodation:	pilot, navigator, bomb aimer/gunner and flight engineer/gunner
Dimensions:	
Length:	51ft 10in. (15.8m)
Wingspan:	59ft 1in. (18m)
Height:	15ft 0in. (4.56m)
Weights:	
Empty:	11,486lb (5,210kg)
Max T/O:	19,482lb (8,837kg)
Performance:	
Max Speed:	255mph (410km/h)
Range:	628 miles (1010km)
Powerplant:	two BMW-Bramo 323P Fafnir engines
Output:	1,972hp (1,472kW)
Armament:	
Up to eight MG 15 7.92mm machine guns in nose, rear upper cockpit, cockpit sides and ventral gondola; maximum bomb load of 2,205lb (1,000kg) in bomb-bay.	
Production:	
887 Do 17Zs were built in 1939–40	

THE STRATEGIC SITUATION

After the *Blitzkrieg* in the West and the evacuation of troops from Dunkirk in Operation *Dynamo*, Britain faced a perilous situation. Quite clearly, Germany's intent was to either militarily neutralise or else to occupy the British Isles, and the key to any such plan was the achievement of air superiority over the RAF. In order to carry this plan forward, of course, almost the entire fighting strength of the Luftwaffe was moved into position on the occupied coastlines of Europe facing Britain. Once those forces were organised into *Luftflotten* 2, 3 and 5, so offensive operations against Britain began in earnest during late June and July 1940. Broadly speaking, the units involved were based in northeastern France, Belgium and the Netherlands (*Luftflotte* 2), northwestern France (*Luftflotte* 3) and Norway (*Luftflotte* 5).

Although the Luftwaffe lacked any long-range heavy bombers, its huge medium bomber force was now within easy range of all of the British Isles. In fact, virtually the entire frontline operational strength of the Luftwaffe was now ranged against Britain, concentrated throughout all the occupied countries of northwest Europe. Crucially, all the key targets for the Luftwaffe were in London and southeast England, and they too were also now within range of escort fighters that could offer protection to the bomber force.

Although RAF Fighter Command had gained knowledge and experience in dealing with German bombers during the *Blitzkrieg*, it was now facing a far more serious test. More than 500 British fighters (mostly Hurricanes) had also been lost during the fighting in France, the Low Countries and over Norway. In France alone, the RAF had had 453 fighters destroyed and 534 pilots killed, missing,

OVERLEAF
RAF Fighter Command sector and fighter airfields in southeast and southern England during the Battle of Britain.

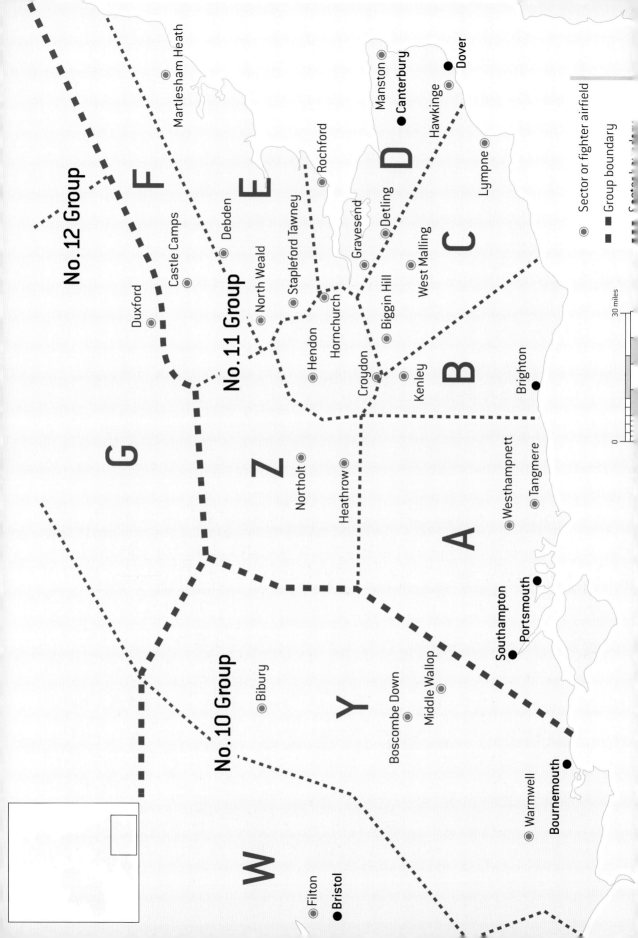

No. 12 Group

No. 11 Group

No. 10 Group

F

E

D

C

B

A

G

Z

Y

W

Martlesham Heath

Castle Camps

Debden

Duxford

North Weald

Stapleford Tawney

Rochford

Hendon

Hornchurch

Croydon

Gravesend

Biggin Hill

Detling

West Malling

Kenley

Manston

Canterbury

Dover

Hawkinge

Lympne

Brighton

Northolt

Heathrow

Westhampnett

Tangmere

Southampton

Portsmouth

Bibury

Boscombe Down

Middle Wallop

Warmwell

Bournemouth

Filton

Bristol

Sector or fighter airfield

Group boundary

30 miles

0

A typical east coast CH radar station during the Battle of Britain period, clearly showing the metal girder construction transmitter masts and the smaller wooden lattice-work receiver masts. There were 22 such stations in total in 1940. (Author's Collection)

wounded or captured. However, RAF pilots now had several distinct advantages over their Luftwaffe counterparts that helped offset their numerical disadvantage. Firstly, they were, in the main, fighting over home territory, with little risk of capture if shot down. Secondly, they were fighting within the umbrella organisation of an integrated air defence system (the 'Dowding System') that provided the command and control structure which had been so sorely missing during the fighting across France and the Low Countries.

RAF Fighter Command was organised into Nos. 10, 11, 12 and 13 Groups during the Battle of Britain, and it had a total of 644 frontline fighters spread amongst 71 frontline squadrons and units (including two from the Fleet Air Arm) when the battle officially began on 10 July 1940. The squadrons of Nos. 10, 11 and 12 Groups in the south, southeast and east of England primarily faced the greatest weight of Luftwaffe attack.

The command and control system was very much the 'ace of trumps' for the defending RAF fighter force. Its backbone was an established chain of some 48 radar stations that was in place by July 1940 within a CH and CHL system stretching clockwise along the coast from the Shetland Islands around to southwest Wales. These radar stations, part of the RAF's No. 80 (Signals) Group, were able to give early warning of the approach of hostile aircraft. In the case of the CH stations, aircraft at medium or high altitude could be tracked at ranges of more than 100 miles, although aircraft or formations below 5,000ft could not be tracked by CH.

Consequently, a network of CHL stations were established during late 1939, and these could detect

The Hopton-on-Sea, Norfolk, CHL (Type 2) radar mast, with its transmitter/receiver aerial located on top of the Caledon Mk II rotation gear. Such sites were early targets for Ju 87s during the initial phase of the Battle of Britain. (Author's Collection)

aircraft at 2,000ft flying some 35 miles from the coastline. However, the radar network could only 'see' incoming hostile raids as they approached the coastline, so once they had passed behind the stations the radar network was blind. However, a contingency for this 'blind spot' in the form of the Observer Corps was already a crucially vital part of the command and control system.

The Observer Corps had an established network of observer posts the length and breadth of the country that were manned 24 hours a day by volunteers. They would plot the passage of incoming raids, with this information being fed into Fighter Command's system as a vital part of Britain's air defence. How it all worked and meshed together was a masterpiece of ingenuity, and at the time was the world's only integrated fighter command and control system, of which Prime Minister Winston Churchill would later say:

When enemy aircraft travelled inland from the coast, they passed behind the CH and CHL stations and became invisible to radar. It was then up to the Observer Corps to plot the raid's progress. Here, a two-man team atop a building in London monitor the progress of an incoming raid using an Observer Post Instrument – a mechanical sighting instrument mounted over a gridded map. This proved to be a vitally important piece of equipment during the Battle of Britain. (Author's Collection)

All the ascendancy of the Hurricanes and Spitfires would have been fruitless but for this system which had been devised and built before the war. It had been shaped and refined in constant action, and all was now fused together into a most elaborate instrument of war, the like of which existed nowhere else in the world.

The information from the coastal radar stations was fed by landline into a Filter Room at the HQ of RAF Fighter Command, Bentley Priory, and from here directly

WAAF plotters and tellers sit facing the General Situation Map within the No. 11 Group Operations Room at RAF Uxbridge, Middlesex, in the summer of 1940. It was their job to move raid markers and counters around the map board. Immediately behind the curved glass screen at the top of the photograph is the duty controller's dais. (Author's Collection)

into the adjacent HQ Operations Room. The latter was dominated by a General Situation Map (GSM) that allowed the duty controller to assess the threat posed to each of the groups in RAF Fighter Command and to allocate each 'raid' to the most appropriate group.

With a specific threat allocated down the chain of command to the relevant Group Operations Room (which would also be receiving incoming information via the Filter Room, displayed on its own GSM), the Group Controller would be able to allocate the hostile plots to the most appropriate sector within his group. Again, the Sector Controller would have his own GSM on which all the information relevant to his sector was displayed, and he would 'scramble' fighters directly under his jurisdiction, on the command of Group HQ, and then control them onto the incoming hostile plots. The information available to the Sector Controller would be further enhanced by immediate information being directly fed to him from Observer Corps posts, as well as information from RAF Direction Finding stations that would be keeping track of the relative positions of friendly fighter aircraft.

With this detailed information, the Sector Controller could guide his fighters in the most advantageous manner, generally positioning them so that they attacked from out of the sun and, *ideally*, at a higher altitude than the enemy aircraft. However, although pilots always wanted to have the advantage of height, it was not always possible to get the defending fighters to such an altitude quickly enough. In fact, it is recorded that on no fewer than 30 occasions between 8 and 18 August, for example, the Luftwaffe not only had the advantage of numbers, but also of altitude. The reasons for this were varied.

Firstly, although the radar stations were detecting the approach of the enemy, they frequently failed to make any estimate of height and, when they did, it was frequently an underestimate. Secondly, the marks of Spitfire and Hurricane then in service took between 18 and 21 minutes to reach 25,000ft, by which time enemy fighters were usually waiting for them. Thirdly, a controller's orders had to take into account meteorological conditions, for he could not afford to risk sending his squadrons so high that an enemy formation could slip beneath them under the cover of cloud. Typically, bomber formations would fly at around 15,000ft and, often, very much lower than that. The aircraft likely to be at 25,000ft, or higher, would generally be the top cover escorting fighters, waiting to pounce on any RAF fighters interfering with their charges below.

Clearly, the main target for British fighters was always the bomber force, and given that this is the context of this book, it is certainly necessary to look at what is, to a degree, something of a myth – that Hurricanes were generally 'detailed' to deal with the bombers, and Spitfires the fighters. Commenting on this supposition, Sqn Ldr Anthony Norman, a Sector Controller at RAF Kenley, Surrey, during the Battle of Britain, said:

> It is important to emphasise that it was *never* the case that Hurricanes were specifically despatched to deal with the bombers and the Spitfires to engage the fighters, although it is often suggested that this is what happened. That notion is complete rubbish because it was impossible, tactically, as we just didn't know, anyway, how the raid being

Luftwaffe bomber bases

Soesterburg
KG 4
He 111

NETHERLANDS

Le Culot **KG 3**
Do 17

Brussels
KG 30
Ju 88

BELGIUM

Stavanger (Norway)
KG 26
He 111

NORTH
SEA

Laon **KG 77**
Ju 88

Lille-Nord
KG 53
He 111

Arras
KG 2
Do 17

Montdidier
KG 1
He 111

Paris

Cormeilles-en-Vexin
KG 76
Do 17

Orly **KG 51**
Ju 88

Villacoublay
KG 55
He 111

Orléans/Bricy
LG 1
Ju 88

Evreux
KG 54
Ju 88

Tours
KG 27
He 111

London

English Channel

FRANCE

Caen
StG 77
Ju 87

Falaise
StG 1
Ju 87

GREAT BRITAIN

St Malo
StG 2
Ju 87

Dinard
StG 3
Ju 87

Vannes
K.Gr 100
He 111

Brest
I./KG 40
Fw 200

N

0   40 miles

intercepted was made up. We had no way of knowing if it comprised fighters, or bombers, or both. So, at Kenley we could end up sending No. 615 Sqn's Hurricanes against fighters and then No. 64 Sqn's Spitfires off after a bunch of bombers. It had to be that way.

However, this observation might be seen to somewhat fly in the face of specific instructions issued by Air Vice Marshal Keith Park, Commander-in-Chief No. 11 Group, to his Sector Controllers on 11 September 1940. In part, they stated:

READINESS SQUADRONS: Despatch in pairs to engage the first wave of enemy. Spitfires against the fighter screen, and Hurricanes against bombers and close escort.

However, this does not address the issue raised by Sqn Ldr Norman, which was simply that the Controller had no means of knowing how the formations being intercepted were made up until the squadrons established visual contact. At that stage, it may have been possible for units to engage more appropriately by fighter type but, very often, it was then too late for Spitfires and Hurricanes to engage as Park had directed. That said, it may well be that Park had intended Controllers to draw an assumption that plots showing at 25,000ft+ might reasonably be expected to be fighters, and those coming in at significantly lower altitudes might be expected to be bombers. Unfortunately, the flaw in any such plan was the frequent failure or inability of radar to accurately predict the height of incoming raids. And neither was it the case that the relative altitudes of plots necessarily indicated the formation's composition anyway.

Notwithstanding the occasional failings of the early warning system, the command and control structure held up well and worked, generally, exactly as was intended and planned. With relatively few modifications, the system remained in place throughout the war, and offered the model upon which subsequent fighter control systems were based and developed. Without it, RAF Fighter Command could not have dealt adequately with the Luftwaffe's bomber formations.

OPPOSITE
Luftwaffe bomber units generally operated with I., II. and III. *Gruppen*. Because of the size of these overall units (each *Gruppe* was smaller than an RAF wing but appreciably larger than a British squadron), usually with three *Staffeln* (each the size of a typical 12-aircraft RAF squadron) in each *Gruppe*, it was mostly impossible to base all aircraft at a single airfield. Thus, they were almost always based geographically close to each other. The locations shown on this map give a good idea of the spread of Luftwaffe bomber bases across France, Belgium and the Netherlands. They are also given as the airfield where the HQ/*Stab* units were based. Those bases also generally accommodated at least one other *Gruppe* of the unit, often the I. *Gruppe*. It is also important to note that sometimes these units moved location, but this map shows the bomber *Geschwaderen* (each the size of an RAF wing) at the bases they occupied for the greater part of the Battle of Britain.

Pilots from No. 19 Sqn stage a mock 'scramble' from the back of a truck at RAF Fowlmere, near Duxford, on 1 September 1940. Although assigned to No. 12 Group, the unit saw considerable action in the skies over neighbouring No. 11 Group. (Author's Collection)

THE COMBATANTS

During 1940 generally, and the Battle of Britain specifically, the fighter pilots of the RAF and the bomber crews of the Luftwaffe who faced each other in combat were among the most highly trained fliers to see action during World War II. In the case of the RAF, especially during the early stages of the battle, many of them were experienced career officers or NCO pilots. Others were drawn from the RAF Volunteer Reserve and were often well-trained civilian pilots. That said, and however good their training, they did not yet have combat experience when first thrown against the Luftwaffe in 1939–40.

In this same respect, many of the Luftwaffe's aircrew during 1940 were already seasoned combat veterans. If they had not seen action during the Spanish Civil War they might have participated in the Polish campaign of September 1939 and, at the very least, benefitted from the knowledge and experience gained in action by their peers who had 'been there and done it'. Experience of the reality of modern air fighting was the most valuable asset to have during the summer of 1940, and there could be no substitute for experience over theory.

RAF pilots had no such comparable experience base to draw upon. All they had was the perceived wisdom handed down by successive generations of fighter pilots since 1918, and the rigidity of inflexible formation tactics that required fighters to fly in fixed groups that saw them formate on the leader. This meant that only the leader was able to freely look around the sky, whilst the remaining ten or eleven pilots concentrated on holding formation. This policy, of course, along with specific instructions as to how aerial combat was to be conducted, was dictated in pre-war *Air Publications*, notably *Air Fighting Tactics* (1938). All of it, however, was simply theory, and the Germans had already learned through experience what the best practice for air fighting might be. For example, by the late 1930s the Luftwaffe had established that a flexible 'finger-four' formation was the best offensive and defensive grouping for fighters, although it did not take long for the RAF to realise the failings of the rigid formation once it entered combat over France.

Indeed, as early as June 1940, RAF Fighter Command noted that Luftwaffe fighters in combat 'normally operate in pairs. If two pairs are flying together prior to combat they usually fly in a finger-four formation' (that is, positioned as if each aircraft were at the tip of each finger on an imaginary outstretched hand). However, it was very much left to individual RAF fighter squadrons to work out their own tactics once it became clear that the so-called 'Hendon Air Pageant' formations were not only not working, but also resulting in the loss of pilots and aircraft. Nevertheless, some squadrons would rigidly stick to what the training manuals had instructed.

As units began to adapt in reaction to their experiences, there was no overall policy laid down as to how fighter formations should be flown. It very much evolved on a squadron-by-squadron basis. For example, by the end of the Battle of Britain, Nos. 66, 74, 92, 501, 602 and 605 Sqns (a mixture of Spitfire and Hurricane units) were all doing things differently, particularly when climbing to intercept. No longer were squadrons forming up on the leader, but instead throwing away the rule book and adapting.

For instance, with No. 66 Sqn, a pattern of three formations, each of four aircraft, was flown, the idea being that the unit could then immediately form into pairs if suddenly attacked. With No. 74 Sqn, a similar three–four pattern was operated and flown in three columns, side by side, and with the centre column slightly to the fore. Meanwhile, No. 605 Sqn climbed in vics astern to 'keep the squadron compact and facilitate cloud flying', with the unit reporting that the formation was 'totally offensive, highly manoeuvrable, easily able to meet attack at any point and well-guarded against surprise'. The latter point was something that all squadrons had now learned – the need to guard against surprise attack, and a possible 'bounce' out of the sun.

In fact, and notwithstanding the variety of formations flown as squadrons went into battle, all of them had a 'weaver' who would fly a reciprocal pattern, to-and-fro, above and behind the formation on the lookout for a surprise attack. Rather than rely on a singleton weaver, some squadrons would put a section of three aircraft on the task. Sometimes, though, it was the weaver(s) who was picked off, first, without having seen the attacker he was on the lookout for.

However, the whole point of fighter interceptions was to attack, disrupt and destroy the bomber formation, and whilst an escorting fighter attack needed to be guarded against, it was the bombers that the RAF fighters were principally after. Quite apart from the differing formations flown as the squadrons climbed, patrolled or went into battle, the actual fighter attack methods employed once the fighters had sighted the

Spitfire Is of No. 19 Sqn climb away from RAF Duxford during a pre-war Battle Formation exercise. This tight formation was subsequently employed by Fighter Command for much of the Battle of Britain. The rigid adherence to such unwieldy tactics by the RAF saw a number of Spitfire and Hurricane units sustain heavy losses to marauding Bf 109Es during the campaign. (Tony Holmes Collection)

Fighter Attack No. 1

RAF Fighter Command had laid-down procedures for tackling enemy bombers, and this is a diagrammatic representation of Fighter Attack No. 1.

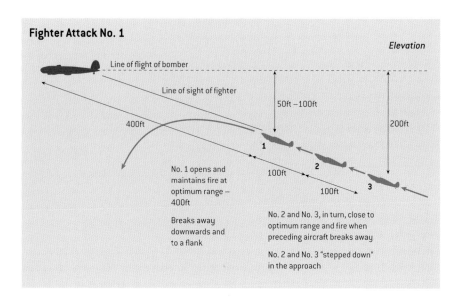

Fighter Attack No. 1

Elevation

Line of flight of bomber

Line of sight of fighter

50ft –100ft

400ft

200ft

1

2

100ft

3

100ft

No. 1 opens and maintains fire at optimum range – 400ft

Breaks away downwards and to a flank

No. 2 and No. 3, in turn, close to optimum range and fire when preceding aircraft breaks away

No. 2 and No. 3 "stepped down" in the approach

bombers remained set. In RAF parlance, these were standard Fighter Attacks Nos. 1, 2 or 3. Additionally, the Air Ministry set out detailed instruction in respect of the overall policy of attacking escorted bomber formations, thus:

Fighters versus Escorted Bombers
1. It is essential that leaders should weigh up the situation as a whole before delivering attacks. Rushing blindly in to attack an enemy may have disastrous results and will certainly be less effective.
2. Never fly straight, either in the formation as a whole or individually. When over enemy territory, alter course and height with a view to misleading A.A. [anti-aircraft artillery]
3. Keep a constant watch to the rear of the formation of aircraft.
4. Upon hearing close gun fire, turn immediately. Hesitancy in so doing may result in effective enemy fire. Do not dive straight away.
5. Before taking off, search the sky for enemy fighters, and if they are known to be about, turn as soon as possible after taking off. Enemy fighters have frequently dived on aircraft whilst taking off from their aerodrome. Similar remarks apply during landing.
6. Conserve ammunition as much as possible. A short burst at effective range is usually decisive and leaves further ammunition for further attacks.
7. Exploit surprise to the utmost. The enemy has been taught to do this, and you should be prepared accordingly.
8. Always remember that your objective is the ENEMY BOMBER.

Much of the entrenched attitude to formations and tactics referred to in the paragraphs on page 44 may well have been attributable to the fact that, at this stage of the war, many fighter squadrons were being led by commanding officers (COs) who had been appointed by dint of age, experience and seniority within the service. The fact of the matter was that all these elements militated against such COs and their success (or lack of it) in leading air fighting.

Fighter Attack No. 2

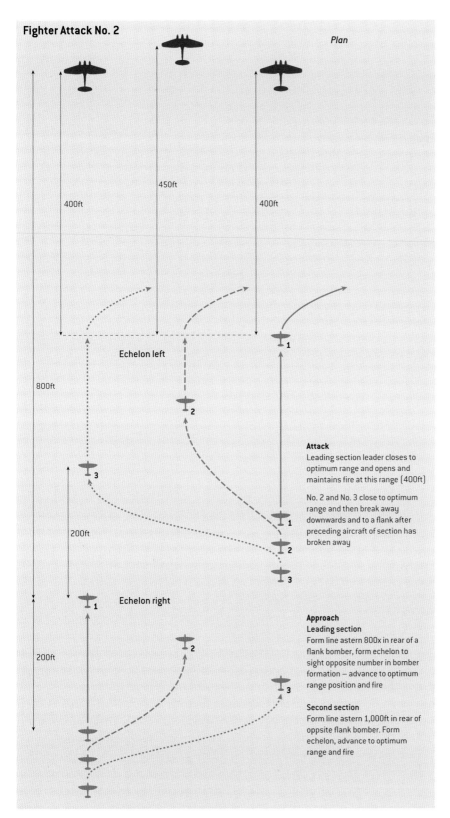

Plan

450ft

400ft

400ft

Echelon left

800ft

Attack
Leading section leader closes to optimum range and opens and maintains fire at this range (400ft)

No. 2 and No. 3 close to optimum range and then break away downwards and to a flank after preceding aircraft of section has broken away

200ft

Echelon right

Approach
Leading section
Form line astern 800x in rear of a flank bomber, form echelon to sight opposite number in bomber formation – advance to optimum range position and fire

200ft

Second section
Form line astern 1,000ft in rear of oppsite flank bomber. Form echelon, advance to optimum range and fire

Fighter Attack No. 2
The theory of Fighter Attack No. 2, seen in plan view.

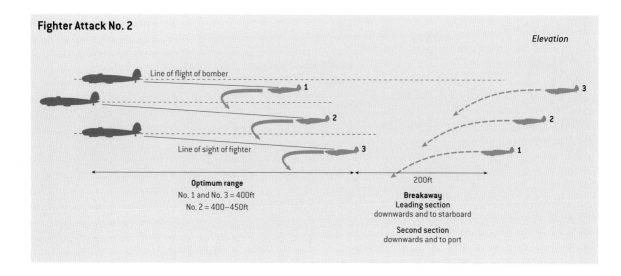

Fighter Attack No. 2

Elevation

Line of flight of bomber

1

2

Line of sight of fighter

3

3

2

1

Optimum range
No. 1 and No. 3 = 400ft
No. 2 = 400–450ft

200ft

Breakaway
Leading section
downwards and to starboard

Second section
downwards and to port

Fighter Attack No. 2

The theory of Fighter Attack No. 2, seen in side view.

In terms of age, these were often pilots well into their thirties or sometimes just beyond – old men in the young man's world of air fighting! In respect to their perceived experience, these leaders may well have been experienced *fliers*, but they had no experience of air combat. As to seniority, herein lay another problem. Being long in the tooth and dyed in the wool, these fighter leaders all had RAF service discipline and the adherence to following orders instilled into them. Thus, the very idea or notion of bucking the system and going against what their training or manuals had instructed could only be anathema to them.

Units who fell into this category often suffered catastrophic casualty rates, an example being Hurricane-equipped No. 257 Sqn. Here, leadership issues, tactics and morale became such a major problem during the summer of 1940 that, by 7 September, its losses were so high the unit's ineffectual CO was removed from his post. In his place, an experienced and younger fighter pilot with leadership qualities was drafted in from his post as a flight commander with another squadron. His name was Flt Lt R. R. S. Tuck, a pilot who would go on to become one of the RAF's most famous aces. It was a similar situation with other frontline fighter squadrons, too. Spitfire-equipped No. 234 Sqn lost its CO on 13 August on what was the very eve of its own part in the battle. In his place, Australian Flg Off Pat Hughes initially took over as almost *de facto* CO until the appointment of another squadron leader on 17 August who, along with Hughes, was killed on 7 September 1940.

In fact, as COs were either killed or posted out, it became the norm for senior battle-experienced flight commanders (almost always of flight lieutenant rank) to be promoted and posted to their own squadron commands. Hence, as the battle wore on, squadron COs became more experienced and capable, although replacements were now coming through a training system that was cutting corners in order to get pilots operational as quickly as possible in order to address the rising attrition rates.

It was also the case, on some squadrons, that NCO pilots were the most 'qualified' in the art of air fighting. This 'qualification' was achieved through experience, such that newly posted commissioned officers, fresh from an Operational Training Unit, would not have had the faintest idea what was going on in aerial combat. It was

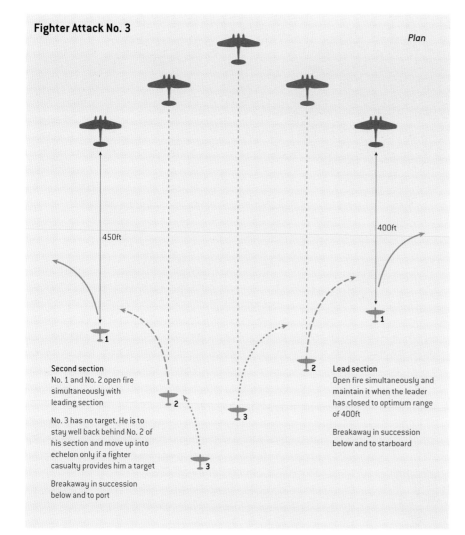

Fighter Attack No. 3

Plan

450ft

400ft

Second section
No. 1 and No. 2 open fire simultaneously with leading section

No. 3 has no target. He is to stay well back behind No. 2 of his section and move up into echelon only if a fighter casualty provides him a target

Breakaway in succession below and to port

Lead section
Open fire simultaneously and maintain it when the leader has closed to optimum range of 400ft

Breakaway in succession below and to starboard

Fighter Attack No. 3
Fighter Attack No. 3 is shown here. All were textbook methods of attack that often could not be conducted 'by the book' by dint of tactical considerations, enemy formations and interference from escorting fighters.

Sqn Ldr Bob Tuck transformed the fortunes of No. 257 Sqn when he joined the unit as its CO in early September 1940. Already a proven ace with 11 and 2 shared victories to his credit following action with No. 92 Sqn, he subsequently claimed a further five kills with his new unit up to the official end of the Battle of Britain. Tuck was very much a 'bomber killer', claiming 16 and 2 shared destroyed between 24 May 1940 and 12 May 1941. (Tony Holmes Collection)

equally the case with flying officers or even flight lieutenants being posted to operational squadrons from non-operational units or fighter squadrons that had been stationed in relative backwaters. Indeed, Hurricane-equipped No. 46 Sqn, for example, was led into action on a number of occasions by Flt Sgt Eric Williams because he was the most experienced fighter pilot in the unit – its pilot officers, flying officers and even flight commander flight lieutenants were all new to air fighting.

It was not only RAF Fighter Command, however, that were posting out ineffectual aircrew, modifying tactics or dealing with

Flying in close, stepped-up, three-abreast formation, He 111s from an unidentified unit cross the Channel and head for southeast England. The aircraft closest to the photographer has distinctive white 'tactical formation' markings in the form of three vertical bars on the outer section of its port wing – these started to appear from late August 1940. The purpose of these markings was to enable pilots to quickly determine the position of other aircraft in the formation. (Author's Collection)

A gunner in a Do 17Z scans the sky for enemy fighters. Armed with a 7.92mm MG 15 machine gun, he could be a dangerous foe even with just a single weapon. (Author's Collection)

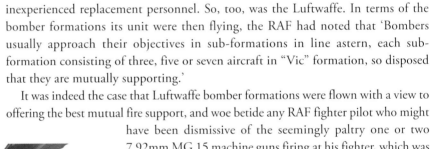

inexperienced replacement personnel. So, too, was the Luftwaffe. In terms of the bomber formations its unit were then flying, the RAF had noted that 'Bombers usually approach their objectives in sub-formations in line astern, each sub-formation consisting of three, five or seven aircraft in "Vic" formation, so disposed that they are mutually supporting.'

It was indeed the case that Luftwaffe bomber formations were flown with a view to offering the best mutual fire support, and woe betide any RAF fighter pilot who might have been dismissive of the seemingly paltry one or two 7.92mm MG 15 machine guns firing at his fighter, which was presenting itself as a small head-on target. The reality was that more than one Hurricane or Spitfire pilot succumbed to just a single well-placed bullet during attacks on bombers.

For Luftwaffe bomber formations, then, the rigid sub-formations noted by RAF intelligence reports did have a very clear purpose – collective defensive fire. And breaking formation would have also broken that mutual protection. Nevertheless, there are reports to be found, contemporary and otherwise, of RAF fighters 'breaking up' formations of German bombers, sometimes in head-on attacks. It is important to address this myth.

In reality, the breaking-up of Luftwaffe bomber formations in this way never really happened, although the famous scene in the 1969 film *Battle of Britain* where a formation of 'He 111s' breaks and scatters across the sky at the approach of Spitfires has likely perpetuated the fable. However, some fighter attacks often did result in single bombers being driven away from the protection of the formation, or falling out of formation through damage. Often, in the case of concerted fighter attacks, several bombers may have dropped out of formation simultaneously, thus giving the impression that they had been scattered. In the case of some head-on attacks, individual bombers took violent avoiding action to steer away from the oncoming RAF fighters, but then re-formed once that imminent danger had passed.

Quite simply, it was essential to maintain cohesion so as to ensure the maximum level of mutual fire support. Fighter protection was not always available or present, and even if it was, the escorts might already be busy tangling with their RAF counterparts and trying to keep them from the bombers. Even so, RAF fighters could still break through, and the bombers needed to defend themselves at all costs. Single bombers that fell out of formation for whatever reason were 'sitting ducks', and they would be picked off should any RAF fighter chance upon them. The bombers would also maintain formation for the run-in to the target and bomb release.

In the case of the *Stukageschwaderen*, however, the actual method of their bombing attacks was necessarily

RAF pilots found Ju 87Bs almost impossible to shoot down in a dive because fighters quickly built up too much speed and shot past their targets. This aircraft, with its underwing dive brakes extended, was photographed moments after its pilot had released his full load of bombs – a single SC 250 and four SC 50s. (Tony Holmes Collection)

different. And how the Stukas went about their deadly business also dictated how RAF fighters dealt with them. For accuracy, it was important that each Ju 87 was heading as near as possible into the wind during its attack dive. As he approached the target, the formation leader looked for smoke rising from the ground, or other clues, to give him the wind direction. He would then align his attack, taking the wind direction into account. Through a window in the cockpit floor immediately in front of his seat, the pilot watched the target slide into position beneath him. When the formation leader commenced his attack dive, the remaining aircraft in the formation followed in turn.

When attacking targets with a small horizontal extent – bridges or small buildings, for example – the Ju 87s approached in echelon formation, peeled into the dive and attacked in line astern. Against larger targets, including ports and airfield hangars, the aircraft would usually be 'bunted' into the dive in three-aircraft *Ketten*, with all three attacking together.

Once the Ju 87 was established in its dive, typically at an angle of 80 degrees, it was almost invulnerable to attack, as Flt Lt Frank Carey of No. 43 Sqn found out:

In the dive [when the Ju 87 could reach 450km/h] they were very difficult to hit because, in a fighter, one's speed built up so rapidly that one went screaming past it. But it couldn't dive forever!

Ideally, of course, the Stuka formations needed to be hit *before* they started their dives. However, their Bf 109 close escort could be a force to be reckoned with on the run-in to a target. On 18 August 1940, for example, there were more than 150 escorting Messerschmitts for Ju 87s attacking targets in West Sussex and Hampshire – more than one fighter per Stuka!

In their fighter protection role for the Stuka, the Bf 109s flew in a mass formation as top-cover to the dive-bombers on approach to the target. As they neared the latter, the fighter formation then split, with one half remaining with the Stukas at altitude whilst the others dived to around 3,000ft to protect the Ju 87s once they had pulled out of their dives. Thus, in theory, the higher formation could cover the Stukas as they attacked their targets, and when the Ju 87s pulled out of their dives at around 1,000ft (often, much lower than that), the lower formation of Bf 109s would already be in position to again protect them from above. However, on 18 August, the defenders managed to catch and shoot down at least four of the Stukas before they commenced their dives. This was just at the point when the high-level escort was at its weakest because half their number had split off to provide the low-level cover.

Pulling out of their dives, the Stuka pilots' tactic was to leave the target area in loose gaggles at cruising speed. If one of their number came under fighter attack, the targeted pilot opened his throttle and accelerated past the dive-bombers in front, thus drawing his pursuer into the fixed wing guns of the Ju 87s he had just overtaken. That, at least, was the theory.

Very often, though, it was a case of *how* attacks were delivered by RAF pilots on individual bombers or bomber formations that would determine the outcome of the engagement – both in terms of the pilot's success and his survival. Again, recent combat experience from France had dictated the new instructions given to RAF fighter pilots during the early summer of 1940 in Fighter Command's Tactical Memorandum No. 8:

All wearing their multi-zippered summer flying suits, pilots and gunners from I./StG 1 gather around a Leutnant holding a map and compass in front of a Ju 87B at Falaise in the early summer of 1940. They have yet to don their bright yellow kapok lifejackets. Stuka pilots were seen as the elite aviators of the Luftwaffe in the lead up to World War II. (Author's Collection)

Whenever possible, fighters should attack enemy bomber formations in equal numbers by astern or quarter attacks from the same level, taking care not to cut the corners when closing to decisive range, and thus presenting a side view target to the bomber's rear guns. They should keep their nose on the enemy and then, when at decisive range, make a deflection if required. If in a good position, a short burst of two or three seconds may well be decisive, but, in any case, this should not be exceeded without breaking away to ensure that an enemy fighter is not on one's tail. If all is well, the attack can be immediately renewed.

Whenever fighters that are attacking bombers receive warning from their upper guard of an impending attack by enemy fighters, they should immediately break outwards. The German fighters frequently dive once in such an attack, and then carry on away from the combat.

Should the fighters not be numerically strong enough to engage the enemy bombers aircraft for aircraft, it will be necessary to 'nibble' from the flanks. Fighters should be most careful not to approach into the 'Vic' of the bomber formation, as this will expose them to effective crossfire.

French experience has confirmed the doctrine of Fighter Command attacks in that simultaneous attacks against compact sections have proved most effective. This method distracts the attention of machine gunners and enables the fighters to benefit from superiority of fire.

Fighter aircraft, when breaking away from a bomber formation, should endeavour to maintain the maximum relative speed. A steep and violent climbing turn results in the air gunner being given a period in which the only relative movement between himself and the fighter is that of an extension of range, and therefore he has practically a point-blank aim at the fighter. The best form of breakaway would appear to be a downward turn, thus keeping up maximum speed and gradually changing the angle of flight paths of the bomber and the fighter.

For the most part, it was very much a case of 'on-the-job-training' for the fighter pilots of the RAF (certainly when it came to tactics), and it was often a matter of adaptation and innovation in the face of actual combat experience. Both sides needed to tailor and alter their tactics to suit the situations they encountered in the face of actual battle, rather than relying on theory or what was learned in training or from instruction manuals. There could, after all, be no real substitute for air combat training other than air combat itself. That said, the pilots and aircrew of both sides had to be put through basic flying training and be taught operational procedures and simple tactics before being sent to frontline units.

LUFTWAFFE PILOT AND AIRCREW TRAINING

In Germany pre-war, and with the resurgence of nationalistic pride and identity, and associated with the rise to power of the Nazi party, there was a corresponding growth of interest in aviation. Technically, there had been a ban on military flying in Germany under the terms of the 1919 Treaty of Versailles, but this was initially circumvented by 'civilian' flying training, mostly on gliders. When the treaty was ultimately openly flouted by the formal establishment of the Luftwaffe in 1936, flying training took on a whole new momentum that saw not only the intake of men who had received rudimentary glider training but, additionally, pilots from *Deutsche Lufthansa*, army personnel and a number of older fliers from the World War I period.

For the prospective pilot joining the Luftwaffe, the first step was six months at a *Fliegerersatzabteilung* (recruit training depot), which was the equivalent to the Initial Training Wings attended by prospective RAF pilots. At the *Fliegerersatzabteilung*, the main emphasis was on drill and physical training, with the 'air' aspect only introduced in elementary lectures on the principles of wireless and map reading. Having completed his initial training, the student pilot moved to a *Fluganwärterkompanie*, where he spent up to two months studying general aeronautical subjects including the theory of flight. Thus prepared, he moved to an A/B *Schule* (elementary flying school), where

Student pilots and their instructors from *Flugzeugführerschule* 6, based at Danzig-Langfuhr, have gathered in front of a Ju 52/3m for a group photograph in the autumn of 1939. During a course lasting six months, prospective twin-engined fighter, bomber and reconnaissance pilots would have logged up to 60 hours of flying time in the Junkers transport and obsolescent early models of the He 111 and Do 17. (Author's Collection)

A would-be gunner takes his turn at target practice in a training rig based on a mid-upper gondola from a He 111, complete with a MG 15 machine gun. The Fahnenjunker is being closely watched by a veteran Obergefreiter at the extreme right. Two other gunners under training are also taking a keen interest in proceedings. (Author's Collection)

he flew light trainer aircraft such as the Klemm Kl 35, Focke Wulf Fw 44 and Bücker Bü 131.

Whilst working towards securing his A2 licence, the pupil received instruction in aerodynamics, aeronautical engineering, elementary navigation, meteorology, flying procedures and morse code. For his B2 licence, he flew aircraft like the Gotha Go 145 and Junkers W 33 and W 44. On successful completion of his B2 training, the trainee pilot had accrued around 150 hours of flying time, and received his *Luftwaffenflugzeugführerschein* (pilot's licence) and *Flugzeugführerabzeichen* (pilot's badge).

Those pilots selected for single-engined fighters or dive-bombers now went straight to the respective specialist schools for training in these roles. Prospective twin-engined fighter, bomber and reconnaissance pilots were sent to the C *Schule*, however, where they logged a further 50 to 60 hours of flying during a course of some six months' duration. These pilots were given ground training in advanced aeronautical subjects and flew obsolescent operational types such as (in the case of bomber pilots) early versions of the He 111, Ju 52/3m and Do 17. Upon graduating from the C *Schule*, the pilot was now able to fly his aircraft by day or by night with reasonable proficiency, had limited training in instrument flying and could perform simple cross-country navigational flights under fair weather conditions.

On leaving the C *Schule*, bomber pilots received up to 60 hours of extra training in blind flying, before moving to specialist schools. At the latter, fledgling bomber pilots joined up with their crews and commenced combined training, flying in operational types of the latest design. On completion of training at the specialist school, the crew usually remained together, having bonded as a team, and was sent to an operational unit.

However, unlike the RAF, in the Luftwaffe it was not always the pilot who was captain of the aircraft. Indeed, the role of the Beobachter (observer) was not just that of navigator as is often thought. In fact, the observer was trained as an aircraft captain, having flown as a pilot up to C standard before moving to the observers' school for a nine-month course, where he received further tuition in blind flying, as well as navigation. On occasions, then, the Beobachter would be the captain of a bomber.

Having passed through specialist training schools, crews were sent to *Ergaenzungseinheiten* (operational training units) attached to frontline *Geschwader* or *Gruppen*, where they learned the tactical methods of the operational units they were to join. As well as operational training units, the *Ergaenzungseinheiten* served as holding posts for trained crews until they were required by the frontline units as attrition replacements.

From the time he joined the Luftwaffe until he arrived at his *Ergaenzungseinheit*, a bomber pilot had undergone 20 months of training and logged some 220 to 270 flying hours. This figure had typically passed the 300 hours mark by the time he was deemed to be fully operational.

RAF FIGHTER PILOT TRAINING

Before recruits selected for aircrew training got anywhere near an aircraft, they first had to endure the rigours of an Initial Training Wing (ITW). For many Battle of Britain aircrew, this meant being sent to either No. 4 ITW at Bexhill-on-Sea, East Sussex, or to No. 5 ITW at nearby Hastings, also in East Sussex. Here, recruits were put through the paces of basic training – drill, PE, rifle practice and generally learning about the disciplines of service life. Both ITWs were accommodated in a series of seafront hotels, flats and large houses that had been vacated and commandeered for the duration of the war. Drill, PE and route marches were frequently conducted up and down deserted, windswept, promenades and along a coastline over which many of them would very shortly be doing battle.

From an ITW, recruits would be posted out to various Elementary Flying Training Schools (EFTSs). Here, both theory of flight and flying instruction was undertaken usually on the de Havilland Tiger Moth or the Blackburn B-2. Whilst at the EFTS, the trainee pilot would make his first solo flight. This was typically following seven or eight hours of dual instruction. From here, trainee pilots would move to a Flying Training School (FTS) and, at this stage, they would progress to the Miles Master and/or North American Harvard. These were aircraft with performances a little closer to the Spitfires or Hurricanes they might expect to

Initial flying training for a RAF fighter pilot took place in the DH 82 Tiger Moth or Blackburn B-2, and accidents were commonplace. Future No. 73 Sqn Hurricane pilot Plt Off Roy Marchand undershot his landing in N6625 and hit a hedge at Princes Farm near Selston, Nottinghamshire, on 22 May 1939. The aircraft, from No. 30 Elementary and Reserve Flying Training School at Burnaston Aerodrome, Derbyshire, was damaged beyond repair. A veteran of the Battle of France, Marchand was killed in action over Maidstone, Kent, on 15 September 1940. (Author's Collection)

Recently arrived Master Is form an impressive backdrop for student pilots and their instructors of No. 5 Service Flying Training School at a damp RAF Sealand, Flintshire, in late 1939. By May 1940 the unit was equipped with 45 Master Is, as well as a handful of Hawker Hart biplanes and 63 Airspeed Oxford twin-engined trainers – both types visible behind the Miles aircraft. Many of the pilots seen here went on to fight in the Battle of Britain. (Author's Collection)

fly operationally in the event that they were 'streamed' to Fighter Command.

Should he complete his stint at FTS satisfactorily, the trainee would at last be awarded his coveted 'wings', officially the Flying Brevet, and be posted to an Operational Training Unit (OTU) for final training on either Spitfires or Hurricanes. There were, of course, no dual-control versions of either fighter, and it was thus expected that the novice aviator would first simply read the pilot's notes, be shown around the cockpit controls and then make his first tentative solo flight in a Spitfire or Hurricane. Although flying such a powerful fighter for the first time might appear to have been a daunting prospect, Sgt Ken Campbell (a veteran of combat in Hurricanes with No. 73 Sqn in France in the spring of 1940 and an OTU instructor during the Battle of Britain) felt otherwise, 'If a student could pilot a Tiger Moth from a flying and handling perspective, then he should have had no trouble, really, in handling a Spitfire or a Hurricane'.

Instructors at OTUs were generally operational fighter pilots who were being 'rested' from frontline service and, for the most part in 1940, had seen service in France. Thus, they were able to pass on the benefit of knowledge gained in real fighting, rather than what it said in the textbooks. Under their mentoring, at least, newly fledged rookie fighter pilots could be taught the deadly art of fighting in the air by the men who knew best how to do it.

The attrition rate for trainee and novice pilots killed whilst undergoing flying training (at all stages) was significant during the period that RAF Training Command was working at an increased pace trying to keep up a supply of replacement pilots. There was undoubtedly a diminution in the performance of newly trained pilots as corners were cut in order to get them into the frontline quickly to replace operational losses (as well as the toll of casualties from the Battle of France), which were having a serious impact on the capabilities of squadrons in RAF Fighter Command.

On posting to a squadron, the pilot would generally first be sent out on 'Sector Reconnaissance Sorties' in order to familiarise himself with the airfield, the area of operations and with the squadron aircraft. When the squadron CO was satisfied that a pilot was combat-ready, he would be placed on the roster for duty and to stand at readiness – thereafter, being expected to take his place on scrambles or patrols. Usually, this would follow a period of dual flying with the CO in the squadron's Master communications aircraft in order to assess the new pilot's general flying abilities. Once the pilot had been committed to his first operational sortie, it was, quite literally, a baptism of fire. Many new pilots came to their first squadrons with very few flying hours and little experience, especially on type. Some did not even survive their first operational sortie.

A number of pilots were also seconded from different Commands (Coastal, Bomber and Training) to make up the shortages in RAF Fighter Command at the height of the

Battle of Britain. Additionally, several Fleet Air Arm pilots also found themselves posted to RAF Fighter Command squadrons. In these instances, a brief course at an OTU to familiarise 'on-type' preceded postings to operational fighter squadrons. However, and despite the overall attrition rate, there was never a shortage of volunteers for aircrew duties.

In the context of training, it is also important to look at what were known as Fighter Command's 'A', 'B' and 'C' squadrons – a system in place from 1 September 1940. The 'A' squadrons were all of those in No. 11 Group and at RAF Duxford, Cambridgeshire, and RAF Middle Wallop, Hampshire. These units were at the sharp end of the battle, and were generally expected to remain there until the weather broke or the enemy buckled. Some, however, rotated in and out of the main battle area in that period – Nos. 43 and 607 Sqns, for example. The 'B' squadrons comprised the rest of those in Nos. 10 and 12 Groups. These would be kept at full operational strength and support the units in the adjacent No. 11 Group if called upon to do so.

The 'C' squadrons were, effectively, 'reserve' squadrons relegated to the quieter backwaters of No. 13 Group. Here, they pretty much became training squadrons, with pilots often posted to them from OTUs so they could receive first-hand training from a cadre of battle-hardened aviators on an operational squadron that was not in the frontline. The 'C' squadrons could be quickly upgraded to 'A' status whenever required. A typical example of a 'C' squadron was No. 43 Sqn after being posted to RAF Usworth, near Sunderland, from RAF Tangmere on 8 September following heavy losses. Here, it received a steady stream of pilots from OTUs and continued in this role until June 1942, by which time an astonishing 87 pilots had been posted in for training.

These, then, were the basic elements of the training for a RAF fighter pilot up to fully operational standards in 1940.

Sgt Lionel Pilkington was a successful Hurricane pilot with No. 73 Sqn during the Battle of France, claiming three and one shared confirmed victories, two unconfirmed victories and two damaged. He was awarded the Distinguished Flying Medal (DFM), and subsequently served as an instructor with No. 7 OTU in the Battle of Britain, during which time he also shot down a Ju 88 over Wales whilst at the controls of a cannon-armed Spitfire IB that had previously served with No. 19 Sqn. Pilkington was killed in action over France on 20 September 1941 while serving as a flight commander with Spitfire VB-equipped No. 111 Sqn. (Author's Collection)

Future air gunners train against a dummy German aircraft with a Boulton Paul 'A' Turret as fitted to the Defiant. The turret was attached to a purpose-built wheeled rig that could be towed out onto the firing range. The rig also boasted its own petrol-driven motor, which supplied sufficient power to allow the turret to function as if it was installed in a Defiant. (Author's Collection)

WALTER STORP

Walter Storp was born in Schnecken, East Prussia, on 2 February 1910. He initially joined the Kriegsmarine as an aviator, but transferred to the Luftwaffe in 1934. He then flew Heinkel He 60 seaplanes with *Bordfliegerstaffel* 1/106 and subsequently served as a test pilot at a series of Luftwaffe proving centres. He returned to command *Bordfliegerstaffel* 1/196 in the spring of 1938, but later that year Hauptmann Storp was posted to the Luftwaffe Operations Staff. In 1939, he returned to II./*Lehrgeschwader* 1, and in mid-September of that same year he took over the *Erprobungsstaffel* Junkers 88 (later to become KG 30, the unit responsible for developing the new bomber). In March 1940 he was given command of 8./KG 4.

On the afternoon on 9 April 1940, Storp was credited with the sinking of the Norwegian destroyer *Aeger* in Amoyfjorden off Stavanger. During the Battle of France, he flew a number of missions, mainly against shipping — he and his *Staffel* were credited with sinking 65,000 Gross Registered Tonnes of merchant shipping and one destroyer. However, Storp was wounded when his Ju 88 was damaged in combat on 3 June 1940, forcing him to crash-land at Amsterdam-Schiphol.

There is no mention of him in action during the early stages of the Battle of Britain, so it is possible that Storp took several months to recover from his wounds. Finally, on 12 September 1940, he was given command of II./KG 76, Storp specialising in attacks against important industrial and military targets following this appointment. One such attack took place in the early afternoon of 6 October 1940 when, at 1305 hrs, Storp guided his Ju 88 towards RAF Northolt, to the west of London, and, from a height of just 80 metres, dropped two 500kg and two 250kg bombs, hitting a hangar. He destroyed a Hurricane from No. 303 Sqn and damaged two others, killing pilot Sgt Antoni Siudak and AC2 Henry Stennett, and wounding AC2 Kenneth Boyns. Despite No. 229 Sqn scrambling Hurricanes to intercept the lone bomber, Storp returned to France unscathed.

Storp was awarded the *Ritterkreuz* (Knight's Cross) on 21 May, a day after receiving the *Ehrenpokal* (Honour Goblet). On 31 October he was promoted to Major.

In April 1941 Storp was given command of the Bf 110-equipped fighter-bomber unit *Schnellkampfgeschwader* 210, which acquitted itself very well in the early stages of the campaign on the Eastern Front. Indeed, between 22 June and 26 July 1941 it was credited with destroying 823 aircraft on the ground and 92 in the air, and knocking out 165 tanks, 194 guns, 2,134 vehicles, 52 supply trains and 60 locomotives. Storp would be awarded the *Eichenlaub* to the *Ritterkreuz* (Oak Leaves to the Knights Cross) on 14 July 1941.

In September 1941, he returned to Germany to be a staff officer. Almost exactly a year later, and now an Oberst, Storp returned to command the newly formed KG 6. Initially flying missions against Britain in the Ju 88 once again, he then led the unit to the Mediterranean. Storp handed over command of KG 6 in August 1943, after which he became *Kampffliegerführer Mittelmeer*, coordinating all bomber operations in the Mediterranean. Three months later he became Chief of Staff of IV. *Fliegerkorps* on the Eastern Front, before taking command of Ju 88-equipped KG 76 just prior to the Allied landings in Normandy in June 1944. On 1 November Storp was named *General der Kampfflieger*, and the end of the war found him in command of 5. *Fliegerdivision* in Norway.

Post-war, Storp became an architect, and died in Golsar, Germany, on 9 August 1981.

Walter Storp, seen here as a Major later in the war and wearing his Knight's Cross with Oak Leaves. (Chris Goss Collection)

BASIL WHALL

Basil Whall was born in December 1918 in Lewes, East Sussex, and lived in Amersham Common, Buckinghamshire, before the war, where he worked as a turner. He joined the RAF Volunteer Reserve (RAFVR) in July 1937 and was mobilised on the outbreak of war, going to No. 11 Group Pool, RAF St Athan, in the Vale of Glamorgan, before being posted as a sergeant pilot to No. 605 Sqn (which was in the process of switching from Gladiators to Hurricanes) at Tangmere on 20 September 1939.

In April 1940, Whall was posted to No. 263 Sqn, flying Gladiators, and he accompanied this unit to Norway on two separate occasions. During the second deployment he claimed a Do 17 destroyed during the afternoon of 23 May 1940. He had chased the Dornier for 25 miles before finally opening fire, Whall reporting that his victim crashed west of Harstadt. He in turn had to bail out of his fighter due to a lack of fuel following the lengthy pursuit. Whall returned to Britain aboard a troop transport in June, thereby surviving the loss of much of the squadron when the carrier HMS *Glorious* was sunk by the German battleships *Scharnhorst* and *Gneisenau*.

On 5 July he was posted to Spitfire-equipped No. 602 Sqn at RAF Drem, East Lothian, before moving south with the unit to No. 11 Group at RAF Westhampnett, West Sussex. On 16 August, flying with 'B' Flight, Whall shared in the destruction of a Do 17 off the Isle of Portland, Dorset, and on 18 August he was credited with two Ju 87s destroyed before crash-landing on the water's edge at Elmer Sands, West Sussex, after his Spitfire was badly damaged by return fire from one of the Stukas. On 26 August, Whall shot down two He 111s over Selsey Bill, West Sussex, on 7 September he claimed a Bf 109 over south London and 48 hours later he was slightly wounded in the neck and crash-landed near RAF Tangmere after having claimed a Do 17 destroyed south of Mayfield, East Sussex. On 24 September he was awarded the DFM, and on the last day of that month he shared in the destruction of a Ju 88 and claimed another Junkers bomber as a 'probable' east of Bembridge, on the Isle of Wight.

On 7 October, after having shared in the probable destruction of a Do 17 south of Beachy Head, East Sussex, Whall was hit by return fire from another Dornier and badly wounded. His Spitfire spun into the ground at Court Farm, Lullington, East Sussex, shortly thereafter as he tried to force land the fighter. Suffering further injuries in the crash, Whall died on arrival at Princess Alice Hospital in Eastbourne, East Sussex. He was aged 22. Fifteen days later, on 22 October 1940, Whall's stepbrother Flg Off Peter St John of Spitfire-equipped No. 74 Sqn was shot down and killed by a Bf 109.

Basil Whall, one of the pre-war RAFVR NCO pilots who very much formed the backbone of RAF Fighter Command in 1940, had a total victory tally of seven and two shared destroyed, and one and one shared probable at the time of his death. All but one of his claims had been against bombers or dive-bombers.

Sgt Pilot Basil Whall of No. 602 Sqn in 1940. (Author's Collection)

COMBAT

Bomber killers. Sgt Herbert 'Jim' Hallowes (second from left) was one of the outstanding pilots of No. 43 Sqn during the Battle of Britain, and had already been awarded the DFM for action over France. He was also involved in some of RAF Fighter Command's initial engagements with Luftwaffe bombers over the northeast in early 1940, and was one of three pilots from No. 43 Sqn among the leading bomber killers of the Battle of Britain. Another of those aviators was Plt Off Hamilton Upton (far right), seen here in April 1940 with squadronmates including B Flight commander, Flt Lt Peter Townsend (second from right). (Author's Collection)

Whilst RAF Fighter Command pilots had engaged with Luftwaffe bombers over northeast England and Scotland during the latter part of 1939, it was not until early 1940 that RAF fighters finally managed to bring down an enemy aircraft over English soil (as opposed to British soil) when, on 3 February, No. 43 Sqn Hurricanes flying from RAF Acklington, Northumberland, achieved success against He 111s of KG 26 over the northeast coast.

At 0900 hrs, the unit's Black, Red and Blue Sections had been scrambled to meet a threat detected and approaching across the North Sea. Black Section, comprising Flt Lt P. W. Townsend, Flg Off P. 'Tiger' Folkes and Sgt H. J. L. 'Jim' Hallowes, was vectored south at full speed, with Red Section (led by Flg Off C. B. Hull) and Blue Section (led by Flg Off J. W. C. Simpson) being vectored towards the Tyne and the Farne Islands, respectively. Forty minutes later, and three miles east of Whitby, North Yorkshire, Townsend called 'Tally Ho! Bandit at "two o'clock"!' and wheeled his section around to starboard in a climbing turn after a solitary He 111. Closing fast from below, Townsend and his section riddled the Heinkel with 0.303-in. rounds from stem to stern as the bomber headed inland, with the Hurricanes in hot pursuit. It did not get

far. Finally, the 4./KG 26 aircraft was forced to make a crash-landing at Banial Flat Farm, Sneaton, just inland from Whitby.

During the attack, the bomber's upper gunner had fought back valiantly until he was grievously wounded in the withering hail of machine gun bullets. Eventually, as a PoW, he had to have a badly mutilated leg amputated. Another crew member had been shot dead and two others badly wounded. That anyone had emerged alive from their colander-like Heinkel is little short of miraculous.

As discussed earlier in this volume, it was not always a case of Hurricanes going after the bombers and Spitfires going after the fighters – particularly during the large-scale clashes in the Battle of Britain. On 16 August 1940, elements of He 111-equipped KG 55 were engaged in an operation to bomb the Great West Aerodrome but were caught by RAF fighters over West Sussex, including the Spitfires of No. 602 Sqn up from Westhampnett. The attack on one of the bombers was nothing short of merciless, as the Combat Report of Flt Lt Robert Boyd testifies:

> I was Blue 1 of No. 602 Sqn. I sighted a He 111 approximately 1,000ft above and coming towards us. Blue 1 did a climbing turn and delivered a beam attack, followed by Blue 2, who stopped one motor. Successive attacks were delivered by the section until the enemy aircraft crashed in waste ground approximately four miles north of Worthing. Attacked at 1655 hrs. Landed at 1745 hrs.

The report went on to state that the section had expended 9,000 rounds against their target, and an RAF intelligence report noted 'between 300 and 400 0.303-in. bullet holes in the rear. No armour was perforated. Six machine guns salved and approximately 50 magazines.' Of significance is the note that no armour plating had been 'perforated'. This statement confirms the inability of the RAF's rifle-calibre ammunition then in use to pierce armour plating, the destruction of an enemy aircraft being reliant upon rounds hitting the airframe, engines, fuel tanks or cockpit, and causing critical damage. It was not until well into 1941 and the advent of the Spitfire VB that the Hispano 20mm cannon came more widely into use. A pair of Hispanos had been fitted in a small number of Spitfire IBs during the summer of 1940, these aircraft being briefly used in combat by No. 19 Sqn until persistent issues with gun stoppages caused by jammed shells hastened their replacement by conventionally armed Spitfire IIs.

There was also an 'experimental' installation of cannon in two Hurricane Is supplied to No. 151 Sqn in the early summer of 1940, one with two 20mm weapons (L1750) and one with four (V7360). The twin cannon aircraft was frequently flown on operations

BELOW LEFT
The two types of ammunition in use by RAF fighters of the period were 20mm and 0.303-in. calibre (a link from an ammunition belt is also seen to the right of the latter round). The considerably larger 20mm shell could cause devastating damage, irrespective of whether it was a solid shot or explosive round. However, it could often take multiple strikes by 0.303-in. bullets to cause critical damage to a bomber – although sometimes just a single hit in the right place could be sufficient. (Author's Collection)

BELOW RIGHT
Hurricane I L1750 was one of two 20mm cannon-equipped examples supplied to No. 151 Sqn in the early summer of 1940. The aircraft were regularly flown by B Flight commander, Flt Lt R. L. Smith, who was credited with a Bf 109 unconfirmed destroyed and a Do 17 destroyed in L1750. He also claimed a Bf 109 probable and a second Messerschmitt damaged in V7360, which was the second cannon-armed Hurricane. (Author's Collection)

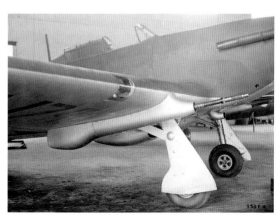

MG 15 7.92mm MACHINE GUN

During the Battle of Britain, the MG 15 was used by all Luftwaffe bomber types as a flexibly mounted defensive weapon. An easy to handle 7.92mm gun that was renowned for its smooth operation, the MG 15 had an open bolt which stayed cocked when the weapon was ready to fire. This meant that the gunner did not have to re-cock it after changing magazines. By pulling the trigger, the bolt released and the magazine was stripped of a round, which was pushed into the chamber. A trip lever then released the firing pin and fired the gun. The discharge recoil would then push the barrel back until the base of the fired cartridge case hit the ejector and flung it out of the receiver. This cycle continued for as long as the operator held down the trigger, with the gun being capable of firing 1,000 rounds per minute. The saddle-drum magazines held 75 rounds, evenly distributed on either side. One magazine would allow a burst lasting about 4.5 seconds. Each gun would usually have a supply of around ten spare magazines.

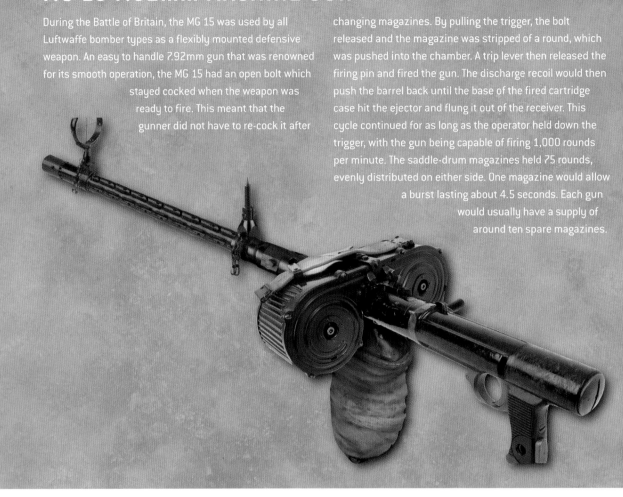

by B Flight commander, Flt Lt R. L. Smith, who explained the difference in the shell sizes between the cannon and the machine gun, and what this meant in combat:

> The comparative size of the 20mm cannon and the 0.303-in. machine gun ammunition was roughly that the 20mm shell was the diameter of a tubular cigar case and the 0.303-in. the diameter of a pencil. Both types had various fillings, 'viz' solid, explosive, tracer. The rate of fire of the cannon was very slow compared to the machine gun – you could almost count the thumps of the cannon, of which there were two or more per aircraft. There were eight machine guns in the Hurricane, and the noise and destructive effect of these weapons all firing at once can be imagined. However, the energy from a machine gun bullet was nothing like that of a 20mm shell, and at say 300 yards, a machine gun bullet had lost most of its penetrative effect against the metal of an aircraft, whereas the 20mm cannon would make a hole in a railway line – consequently, the latter would penetrate the armour behind the pilot's seat, and the casing of the engines.

Despite the Spitfire Is flown by Boyd and his section being exclusively fitted with 0.303-in. machine guns, two of the crew on board the He 111 targeted on

16 August had been killed in the fusillade. The remaining three survived to be captured. Certainly, it must have been terrifying to have been on the receiving end of such firepower, especially when the bomber's only form of defence was one or two MG 15 machine guns – the most common defensive weapon fitted to the Luftwaffe's level bombers and its Ju 87s. However, such odds did not faze Oberfeldwebel Fritz Pons, a radio operator/air gunner with He 111-equipped 8./KG 55 'I had experience against the Spitfire, for instance, using the MG 15. In my opinion, we had a 50/50 chance of winning.'

Oberfeldwebel Fritz Pons, a radio operator/air gunner with He 111-equipped 8./KG 55, created his own bespoke double machine gun mount for the upper gondola of his aircraft. (Author's Collection)

However, even the confident Pons must have realised the shortfalls or inadequacies of just a single 7.92mm MG 15 against eight 0.303-in. Browning machine guns, and he set about creating his own bespoke double mount for the upper gondola of his aircraft. He explained the reasoning behind his contraption:

For one thing, it became necessary to regularly change the saddle drum on top of the MG 15. Each drum carried 75 rounds and gave a total firing burst of 4.5 seconds. It took valuable time to change the drum. You didn't have that time in combat, so I designed and made a double mounting frame to carry two MG 15s instead of the usual single weapon. This meant that I could change over quickly to the other gun if the magazine was empty. This gave me a better chance, I thought. I could also use both guns together for greater firepower if I needed to.

Nevertheless, being a defensive air gunner on board German bombers under attack from RAF fighters was a hazardous occupation, RAF Combat Reports being strewn with comments along the lines of 'I aimed for the gunner to silence him' and 'the gunner slumped down and I saw his gun pointing skywards'. Mostly, the gunners in aircraft being attacked by British fighters had no armour to hide behind. Little wonder, then, that many Luftwaffe bomber crews took to wearing Stahlhelm (steel helmets) over their flying helmets.

As discussed in the previous chapter, Fighter Command's theoretical wisdom for the execution of fighter attacks against bombers was very prescriptively laid down. Largely, an attacking RAF fighter pilot (in a single-seat type), or a squadron or flight commander, would broadly follow that guidance. In the heat of battle, however, the following of written theory would sometimes be impossible, or else be forgotten. Take, for example, the case of Battle of France veteran Flg Off John Hardacre of No. 504 Sqn, who seemed to ignore the 'rules' as he edged closer to a formation of He 111s from KG 55 over the English Channel on 30 September 1940 when the German bomber unit was tasked with attacking the Westland aircraft factory at Yeovil, Somerset. Shot down and killed, his demise was recorded by Feldwebel Robert Götz, an air gunner on board one of the bombers:

ENGAGING THE ENEMY

Like the Spitfire I/II, the Hurricane I was fitted with the Barr & Stroud GM 2 reflector gunsight as standard. This unit, which had been created by the company in 1935, featured a lens through which a large circular graticule was projected onto a circular glass reflector screen 76mm in diameter. The graticule was bisected by a cross, the horizontal bar of which was broken in the centre, with the range/base setting being set via two knurled rings with their own scale that turned a Perspex pointer to various range settings, and an adjustable ring which turned an indicator to wingspan in feet. The internal mechanism then set the gap according to the required range. A central dot was added as a further aiming point.

The pilot first set the span dial to the known wingspan of his prospective target, then the range dial to the maximum for accurate fire. When the target coincided with the gap, it was within range. The radius of the graticule ring gave the deflection allowance for hitting a target crossing at 100mph. The gunsight was illuminated by a half-silvered 12v lamp in a quick release holder at the base of the sight body. A substantial rubber pad was fitted to protect the pilot from injury in the event of a rough landing. Chosen by the RAF as its standard fixed gunsight, the GM 2 was known as the Reflector Sight Mark II in frontline service.

A Hurricane came close to us, as if he was keeping his distance in a formation flight, trying to have a look at us, as if we were quite harmless. Truly a crazy devil. Perhaps he wanted for once to have a really close look at German bombers? The coloured circle on the fuselage flying alongside us took my breath away. Everything then took its natural course, with our small machine guns banging away as hard as they could. And suddenly – to our great surprise – there were flames and smoke streaming out from the unwary intruder. He staggered into a dive and disappeared. So, our small single machine guns, which gave the depressing feeling that they hardly worry the attacking fighters, let alone do any serious damage to them, are after all not altogether useless.

The observations of Götz are interesting on several levels. First, that Hardacre seems to have presented himself as a sitting target for the air gunners. However, it is unlikely (as Götz suggests) that Hardacre was coming close just to 'have a look'. Rather, it is more likely that he was closing in to 'nibble' at the flanks, just as Memorandum No. 8 had suggested, and Götz was certainly on the flank. However, the possibility cannot be excluded that Hardacre had carried out an attack and had not broken away, having thus exposed himself to the air gunners. Either way, the unfortunate pilot (who had claimed four bombers destroyed prior to his demise) discovered to his cost just how dangerous the single MG 15 defensive machine guns on board the German bombers could be – their effectiveness also coming as something of a surprise. In this instance, to Götz himself!

Hauptmann Helmuth Bode, *Gruppenkommandeur* of III./StG 77, runs up the engine of his Ju 87B at Caen, France, during the early stages of the Battle of Britain. The unit's distinctive knight on horseback emblem was based on Bode's family crest. The muzzle of one of the wing-mounted MG 17 7.92mm machine guns can be clearly seen at the extreme right of the photograph. (Author's Collection)

Another RAF memorandum of the period dealt with issues relating to the attacking of Ju 87 dive-bomber formations, noting that the latter were often just a 'disorganised mass of aircraft'. Whilst this may well have appeared to be the case to attacking RAF pilots (especially if delivering attacks just as the Stukas commenced diving onto the target), with the usually stepped-up masses of aircraft seemingly having no form or cohesion, the very opposite was in fact true. There was considerable order to it all.

Hauptmann Helmuth Bode, leader of III./StG 77 in 1940, was one of those, however, who realised there was a flaw in the plan of having formations stepped up in the manner flown by I. and II. *Gruppen* of StG 77, for instance. With those groups, the leader was at the lowest point in the formation, with the following aircraft, in their three-aircraft 'vics', rising one after the other behind him. Bode believed that such a formation prevented the rear gunners from providing the Ju 87s with the most effective defensive cover, since their field of fire above and to the rear was restricted by trailing Stukas. Instead, Bode instigated a formation where the dive-bombers were all stepped *down* on his lead, thus providing gunners with both better visibility to see fighters that were likely to be attacking from above and behind, and giving them an unrestricted field of fire when the Ju 87s were engaged by the enemy. In his words:

We were flying in vee-formations, one *Kette* below the others, so all our rear gunners had a good position with a view to sighting rearwards. With the other two groups, the rear gunners were really limited in where and how they could fire. Upwards, their vision and gunnery was restricted, and they couldn't shoot downwards. All they had was a limited field of fire directly to the rear when in formation. Of course, a fighter pilot would try to attack from the rear and could pick off the rear aircraft, one by one, without the others in the formation being able to do very much to help. In our formation, an attacker from the rear was exposed to many guns in the formation. Thus, the field of fire presented by III./StG 77 was a serious disincentive for attackers.

The effect, in my view, was that our losses were significantly less than those suffered by I. and II. *Gruppen*. That was certainly the case when one looks at and compares the overall casualties suffered by I., II. and III. *Gruppen* of StG 77 on 18 August 1940 – the hardest fought day of the campaign [for the Ju 87], and the worst for Stuka losses. I believed, then, that my own adaptation of tactics was vindicated.

Here, then, was an example of an innovative combat leader making operational decisions in the light of experience and in the face of what were Luftwaffe textbook formation patterns flown, just like the RAF, for operational sorties. Bomber formations did not always have close protection from fighters. Consequently, the adherence to closed formations by Luftwaffe bombers was an essential and integral part of their defence during daylight operations. As with the massed daylight raids carried out by the USAAF later in the war, there was perceived safety – or increased security – provided by concentrated firepower from multiple defensive machine guns. This made attacking groups of bombers riskier when approaching and flying into or through such formations. Helmuth Bode had simply been innovative in determining how to adapt his formations, and thus utilise his limited rearward defensive fire to best effect.

As we have seen, for the most part it was very much a case of 'on-the-job-training' for the fighter pilots of the RAF (certainly in the case of tactics), and it was often a matter of adaption and innovation in the face of actual combat experience. Again, Helmuth Bode's 'adaptations' to the formations flown illustrate that both sides needed to tailor and alter their tactics to suit situations they encountered in the face of actual combat, rather than any reliance on theory or what was learned in training or from instruction manuals.

Thus far, we have looked at actions against German bombers involving Spitfires and Hurricanes. But employing the RAF's two principal fighters against Luftwaffe bombers during the air war over Britain during 1940 is a subject that has been much covered elsewhere, and in this work we are especially focussing on the Defiant versus Luftwaffe bombers. Fighting in the Defiant was unlike anything experienced by the pilots of the Spitfires and Hurricanes of RAF Fighter Command during this period. For one thing, it was not the pilot who did the 'fighting'. He merely had to get his aircraft into a position for his gunner to engage the enemy, its first baptism of fire coming over the French beaches around Calais and Dunkirk as the British Expeditionary Force and Allied troops withdrew, preparatory to Operation *Dynamo*.

During the final week of May 1940, No. 264 Sqn was heavily involved in the fighting over the Channel coast, and on the 29th the Defiant experienced its so-called 'Glory Day'. Unfortunately, subsequent research has taken something of the shine off its achievements, putting into better perspective the reality of events.

Armourers from KG 51 crowd around SC 250 bombs to mark them up with graffiti and messages in chalk before they are loaded on board one of the unit's Ju 88s prior to a sortie over England. (Author's Collection)

That morning, the skies over Dunkirk were quiet due to low cloud over the airfields of both sides. Only at around 1300 hrs did the weather clear sufficiently for serious air operations to begin. At 1445 hrs, led by Sqn Ldr Philip Hunter, 12 Defiants took off from their forward operating base at RAF Manston, Kent, and arrived over Dunkirk at 10,000ft, accompanied by the Hurricanes of Nos. 56, 151 and 213 Sqns at 15,000ft. A hard-fought action ensued, and No. 264 Sqn crews claimed the destruction of eight Bf 109s, nine Bf 110s and a Ju 87 after landing back at around 1630 hrs. Two of its aircraft had, in return, been damaged. The damage inflicted on one of the Defiants had serious consequences many months later when the aircraft crashed following structural failure of the tail unit. Investigations revealed that shoddy battle damage repair following bullet strikes during the action on 29 May was to blame.

Later that day, at around 1900 hrs, No. 264 Sqn again sent 12 Defiants aloft from Manston, the fighters returning to the skies over the French beaches. Here, again flying with the Hurricanes of Nos. 56 and 151 Sqn, and with Spitfires of No. 610 Sqn providing top-cover, the Defiants spotted Ju 87s dive-bombing shipping some 8,000ft below and dived to engage. The Stukas were caught pulling out after their attacks, Sqn Ldr Hunter having perfectly positioned his unit to catch the dive-bombers when they were at their most vulnerable. In a fierce engagement, his gunners claimed 18 Ju 87s and a Ju 88 destroyed, before returning home at 2020 hrs.

Again, over-claiming was rife. In total that day, No. 264 Sqn had claimed 19 Ju 87s destroyed (quite apart from the additional 'bag' of Bf 109s and Bf 110s and a Ju 88), yet the Luftwaffe's total Stuka losses for the 29th were just three. Although over-claiming was often a feature of air fighting, the extraordinarily high tally claimed by the turret fighters might have a credible explanation.

In the case of one-on-one single-seat fighter engagements, the pilot was better placed to make a more objective assessment as to combat outcomes if he followed or watched his victim crash. In the case of Defiant gunners, however, their view was compromised by the heavily framed turret, its guns and aircraft structure. Additionally, he would have been further disorientated as his pilot manoeuvred the aircraft to get away from pursuers, or to position it for an attack on the next target. Meanwhile, the gunner may have been traversing his turret, thus further adding to his spatial confusion. Consequently, his ability to follow an aircraft he had just engaged would have often been severely compromised. Whilst it is most unlikely that the claims in question were deliberately 'optimistic', they were made in difficult circumstances by gunners when observing aircraft going down that they *thought* they had shot at, and that also may have had multiple other attackers, and claimants.

Perhaps the counterpoint to the so-called 'Glory Day' came two months later when, on 19 July, nine Defiants of No. 141 Sqn providing fighter-cover for a Channel convoy were bounced by Bf 109s of JG 51. The attackers came in from behind and below, thus out of reach of the Defiants' field of fire. It was nothing short of a massacre, and the RAF pilots were unable to get their aircraft into a suitable position for the gunners to engage before six of the nine were shot down and ten of the 12 aircrew on board were killed.

The rear turret fairings of all three Defiants seen at Kirton-in-Lindsey in early August 1940 are in the down position to allow maintenance to be carried out on the guns. The aircraft closest to the camera is L7005, which was the most successful Defiant of them all – its crews were credited with 11 and 3 shared victories. It was eventually lost in action on 26 August 1940 while being flown by Sgts Ted Thorn and Fred Barker, who claimed more kills than any other Defiant crew pairing. (Author's Collection)

A formation of Do 17Zs heads for a target in southern England during the summer of 1940. The aircraft fly in *Kette* formation, comprising 'vics' of three Dorniers, which allowed gunners in individual bombers to bring together their collective firepower for better defence against fighter attacks. (Author's Collection)

Fighter Attacks 'A' and 'B'

Attacks 'A' and 'B' were devised for the Defiant to enable the pilot to get his aircraft into an optimum position for his gunner to be able to engage bomber formations. With the Boulton Paul fighter being seen as a dedicated 'bomber destroyer', these methods of attack were conceived as the best theoretical tactics for Defiant formations, although such systems often broke down once combat was joined.

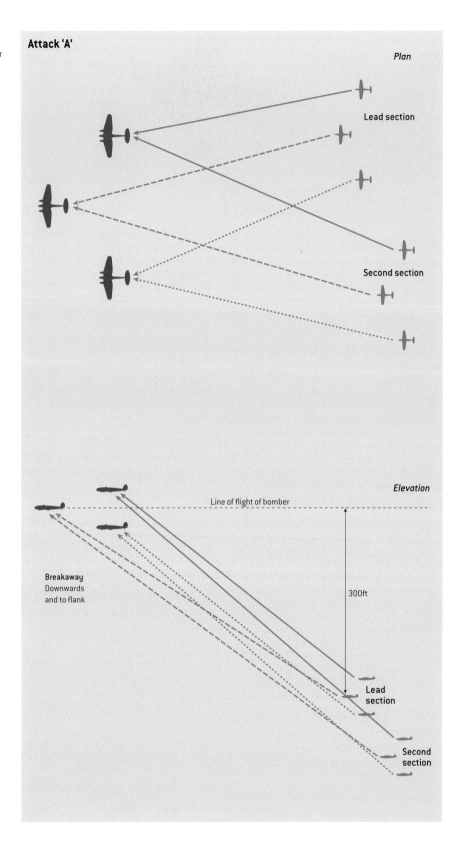

Attack 'A'

Plan

Lead section

Second section

Elevation

Line of flight of bomber

Breakaway Downwards and to flank

300ft

Lead section

Second section

Attack 'B'

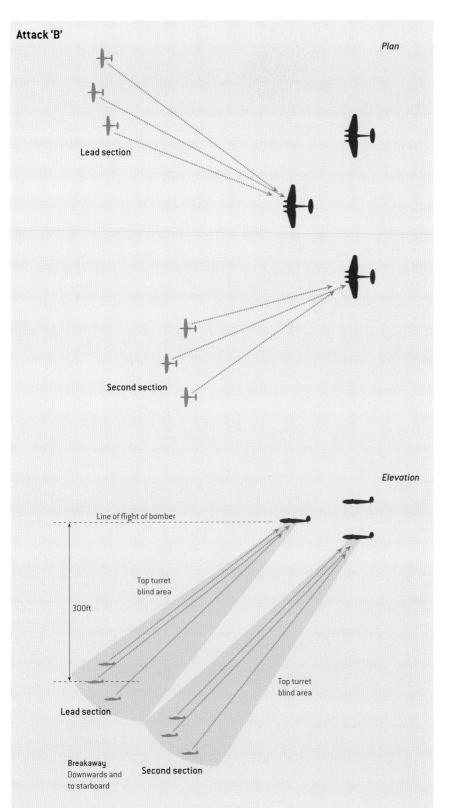

Plan

Lead section

Second section

Elevation

Line of flight of bomber

300ft

Top turret
blind area

Top turret
blind area

Lead section

Breakaway
Downwards and
to starboard

Second section

OVERLEAF

At 1140 hrs on 26 August 1940, No. 264 Sqn was ordered to patrol Dover to intercept approaching enemy bombers. It duly encountered a formation of 12 Do 17s from III./KG 3 at 12,000ft between Herne Bay and Deal, off the east Kent coast, the bombers being escorted by a large formation of Bf 109s.

Sgt E. R. Thorn and his gunner, Sgt F. J. Barker, in L7005/PS-X attacked the Do 17s, hitting one and setting its starboard engine on fire before repeating the performance with another. However, they were then engaged by Bf 109s and their aircraft hit in the radiator and set on fire, although Barker in turn claimed to have downed one of their attackers. Thorn managed to crash-land the badly damaged L7005 at Chislet, Kent, with the Bf 109 they claimed to have destroyed coming down just a few fields away. Both Thorn and Barker were slightly injured. In total, No. 264 Sqn was credited with having destroyed one Bf 109 and six Do 17s, with a seventh Dornier damaged.

Whilst bombers clearly posed the greatest threat to coastal convoys sailing off the east and south coasts of Britain in 1940, the unsuitability of the Defiant in the defence of such convoys had been painfully demonstrated. With luck, and a fair wind, they might see some success against bomber formations if these were unescorted, or if the Defiants could keep away from the fighter screen. Otherwise, the future for RAF Fighter Command's Defiant force (previously perceived as bomber formation destroyers) now looked decidedly bleak in No. 11 Group's 'hot' sectors in southeast England. But the role of the Defiant in the Battle of Britain was not yet over.

One particular claim made by a Defiant crew of No. 264 Sqn has had some resonance in recent years – Do 17Z 5K+AR of 7./KG 3, shot down over the English Channel on 26 August 1940. In this engagement, Plt Off Desmond Hughes and Sgt Fred Gash have been suggested as being responsible for bringing down a Do 17Z that crashed on the Goodwin Sands. It has been stated that this was the same aircraft recovered by the RAF Museum in 2013.

In his unpublished memoirs, Hughes wrote of the action on 26 August which took place at 15,000ft over the East Kent coastline. Having set up his gunner for an attack from beneath the bombers, he described what happened next:

> The specks grew into the long pencil-slim silhouettes of Dornier 17s and suddenly there were the black crosses, insolently challenging us in our own backyard! Fred Gash took as his target the second Dornier and made no mistake – his De Wilde incendiaries twinkled all over it, but particularly on its engine. It began to fall out of the formation, the hatch was jettisoned, two parachutes streamed as little dark figures bailed out and the stricken aircraft went down increasingly steeply, with its starboard engine well alight.

That day, Hughes and Gash were credited with downing two Dorniers, one of them having since been identified as the Goodwin Sands aircraft. The second victory occurred in a chaotic action that followed the initial attack on the formation. Of this second success, Hughes wrote 'Fred had been blazing away at another Dornier', which he later reported as having 'brewed up'. The Defiants were then attacked by Bf 109s, and after shaking them off, Hughes and Gash headed back to base, where they discovered six bullet holes in their aircraft. That night, Hughes sent a telegram to his parents. It said, simply, 'Two up and lots to play.'

Hughes and Gash were credited with downing two Do 17s in that action, one of them having since been speculatively 'identified' as the Goodwin Sands aircraft. However, the latter cannot be the one that Hughes saw two crew bail out of, since that aircraft made a forced-landing on the sands with the crew still on board. The mystery is further deepened by the fact that the recovered aircraft exhibited a bullet strike from dead astern in one of the propeller blades. This does not 'fit' with Hughes' angle of attack from underneath, although it is entirely possible that the bomber was also targeted by other fighters. And it cannot be the one which Gash describes as having 'brewed up', a description typically used to describe a complete destruction by fire and explosion.

In short, the recovered Dornier has, to date, yielded no evidence that it is the machine downed on the Goodwins on 26 August 1940. In fact, and as we have seen, that aircraft landed on the sands at low water, where the notoriously glutinous sand would have quickly swallowed up the bomber on successive tides. That being the case, it is hard to explain how the Dornier – if it is this one – was discovered on its back and on the seabed.

All told, the difficulty in attributing specific 'kills' to specific aircraft is amply demonstrated with this case. So, too, is the difficulty Defiant gunners often had in properly identifying what had happened to aircraft they had shot at. Equally well demonstrated is the vulnerability of singleton bombers in the unfriendly skies over southern England during 1940. In the RAF Intelligence Report on the downed Dornier that landed on the Goodwin Sands, which included PoW interrogation details, it is stated that the aircraft became separated from the formation after the crew lost their bearings. They were then attacked by fighters (plural). Evidence as to the Dornier being on its own also flies in the face of Hughes' assertion that what he had attacked was a group or formation of Do 17s.

Desmond Hughes later recalled, generally, his time with No. 264 Sqn in August 1940:

During the week we were there [at Hornchurch] we lost five pilots and nine gunners. The losses included the squadron commander, the squadron commander designate and both flight commanders either killed or wounded. By mid-day on 28 August there were only two Defiants serviceable and, led by Plt Off 'Dickie' Stokes, the pair of us took off and were vectored towards a raid of 30+ enemy aircraft. Before we reached them, the controller said, 'I'm terribly sorry old boy, but they've turned back. Return to base and pancake [land].' Well, I don't know how the other three chaps felt, but if those 30+ had been Me 109s we would have been in for an interesting time! The next day, the six aircraft that could be made serviceable were flown north to RAF Kirton-in-Lindsey, led by the most senior pilot left on the squadron – 20-year-old Plt Off 'Tommy' Thomas. It hadn't been an auspicious start for my fighting career, or the service record of the poor old 'Daffy', as we sometimes called the Defiant.

That more gunners than pilots had been killed in those August combat losses might have had something to do, in part, with bailing out of the Defiant. Desmond Hughes certainly thought so:

The gunner had a lot of difficulty in getting out. He had an escape hatch in the floor. That was the slow way out. I don't know if anyone ever got out that way. The best way for him to get out was from the rear of the turret, with the pilot turning the aircraft on its back so that both men could fall out.

For ease of exit, however, the gunners were provided with a flying overall or smock arrangement called a Parasuit. Made by the GQ Parachute Company, this ingenious piece of equipment did away with bulky harnesses and packs, and had the 'chute itself incorporated into the seat of the 'coverall' as an integral part of its design. The Parasuit also made sitting in the turret more comfortable, and reduced the risk of straps snagging on the turret on the way out. Indeed, the use of a standard fighter-type seat parachute and harness

He 111H-2 Wk-Nr 2720 of 5./KG 1, having lost a wing in the collision with Flg Off 'Teddy' Morris, plummeted to earth at Swires Farm, Newdigate, Surrey, where four of its seven bombs exploded when the bomber hit the ground. Three of the crew were killed and two captured, with one of the latter being seriously injured. (Author's Collection)

within the cramped confines of the turret would have been an impossibility.

Whether being engaged by Spitfires, Hurricanes or Defiants, the lot of German bomber crews operating in daylight over Britain was certainly a dangerous one in the summer of 1940. What it meant to fly and to fight in a He 111, Do 17, Ju 87 or a Ju 88 during the Battle of Britain is succinctly summed up by Feldwebel Robert Götz, writing about his seventh operational flight over the country in an attack against the Bristol Aeroplane Works at Filton, South Gloucestershire, on 25 September 1940:

Three Me 110 fighter groups have been announced as heavy fighter protection. Over Cherbourg, they suddenly appear above us. It is a very reassuring feeling to see so many big two-engine fighters up there with their shark's teeth and similar symbols painted on them. And these can accompany us much further inland than the Me 109s and are supposed to have terrifying firepower. But there have been rumours that they are by no means all that fast. However, that may be, but there they were as guardian angels, and would soon show their teeth. Up there above Portsmouth the Spitfires are already appearing and attacking savagely. And no counteraction by our fighters is to be seen. This time the flak is too dense.

Now we have been flying over the island for a long while, over mazes of streets, fields, villages and small towns. I am far calmer than during the first flights. In front of the target there is now well-aimed flak again. The puffs cover a wide area, at exactly our height.

A second wave of fighters. Quite a lot this time. With fantastic audacity, and skill of the highest order, they dive between our fighters and ourselves: steep banking, flying upside down, steep turns; firing from all positions and directions. There is a Heinkel already entering the clouds with a Spitfire behind it. With consternation I see a Me 110 flying quite low and slowly over a clear area, when it pulls up sharply. And equally slow, behind it, is a Spitfire, which one can almost see being shaken by the bursts that it is pouring into the body of the battered *Zerstörer*. And above us is flying the main body of our guardian angels, still in unbroken formation. I hadn't seen them in action, whatever others had done. Perhaps, because of their limited capabilities, they had been ordered only to give us some small degree of protection? They obviously have to look after themselves as well. But, in that case, goodbye to daylight attacks on England.

On the return flight, the Tommy fighters are still around us and we are, as usual, accompanied by flak. As we land and clear out the masses of spent drums and cartridge cases, there are 'planes standing near to us with holes as big as a man's head – and even larger. We hadn't a scratch this time. But next time? We all know that it can happen to any of us, any day. This would be very painful for me, but only because of my mother and little brother.

As a testimony of what it was like to fly bomber operations over Britain, against determined defenders, this graphic portrayal in Götz's diary is a powerful narrative. Not only is it an account given in brutal honesty, the diary entry also conveys the dangerous hopelessness of daylight bomber operations over Britain – a hopelessness that had already been recognized by the bomber crews flying these hazardous sorties. Indeed, by the time Götz wrote it in the early autumn of 1940, the RAF's battle against the daylight bomber offensive had been won.

STATISTICS AND ANALYSIS

RAF Fighter Command had fought the Luftwaffe bomber force over Britain since October 1939, when it had first encountered raids by single aircraft, or small groups of raiders (mostly He 111s and Ju 88s), operating across the North Sea and directed towards Scotland and the northeast coastline of England. A number of the fighter engagements against these unescorted raiders were successful, notably those on 17 and 28 October 1939 over the east coast of Scotland by Spitfires of Nos. 602 and 603 Sqns.

By early 1940, such raids were continuing in a somewhat sporadic fashion, but as the war gathered momentum so RAF Fighter Command found itself doing battle with the Luftwaffe's bomber force on a more widespread basis, firstly in Norway, then France and the Low Countries followed by increased air activity against Britain, including the east and southeast. Such activity increased to a peak after the launch of the German *Blitzkreig* on 10 May 1940, and then up to the Dunkirk evacuations in early June. Thereafter, the air assault against Britain gathered further pace, leading to the commencement of the Battle of Britain on 10 July 1940.

Figures taken from the Luftwaffe Quartermaster General's returns of 10 August 1940 show that 3,358 aircraft had been deployed against Britain, of which 2,550 were serviceable. The force comprised 934 single-seat fighters, 289 two-seat fighters, 1,482 medium bombers, 327 dive-bombers, 195 reconnaissance aircraft and 93 maritime aircraft, these totals including the unserviceable aircraft. The number of *serviceable* aircraft amounted to 805 single-seat fighters, 224 two-seat fighters, 998 medium bombers, 261 dive-bombers, 151 reconnaissance aircraft and 80 maritime aircraft.

This He 111P of 4./KG 55 was brought down onto the beach at East Wittering, West Sussex, on 26 August 1940 following attacks by Sgt Basil Whall in a Spitfire from No. 602 Sqn. Only the pilot of the bomber survived, his four crew members being killed in Whall's attacks – the RAF ace claimed two He 111s destroyed on this date. (Author's Collection)

What is interesting about these numbers is that the Luftwaffe had had 1,711 medium bombers at the commencement of the campaign in the West on 10 May, but only 1,482 at the start of the Battle of Britain two months later. The losses sustained by the Luftwaffe in the *Blitzkreig* had been considerable, it being *estimated* that around 1,500 medium bombers had been destroyed in the period from 10 May up to 24 June. Only barely, then, had the Luftwaffe managed to keep pace at all with re-supply and the replacement of aircraft and crews against the attrition rates being suffered.

Although it is impossible to put any exact figure on just how many German bombers fell to RAF fighters during the Battle of Britain, it is certainly the case that a very significant percentage of the losses sustained had been inflicted by RAF Fighter Command. Over-claiming notwithstanding, it is interesting to look at the number of victories credited to the leading 'bomber killers' of the Battle of Britain. From this analysis, it is clear that the majority of claims relating to enemy aircraft destroyed by the leading aces of the day were predominantly for fighters – either Bf 109s or Bf 110s. Most of the top scorers had relatively few bombers included in their overall tallies. Also, one unit boasts the three top 'bomber killers' of the battle – No. 43 Sqn. However, this is perhaps slightly skewed by the multiple claims made by its pilots for Ju 87s destroyed on 16 and 18 August 1940. On the other hand, not included in that top

table are any Defiant crews – somewhat ironic, given that the aircraft was originally conceived as a bomber destroyer.

Of course, though, not all losses suffered by the Luftwaffe were caused by enemy fighters. A number of bombers were brought down by anti-aircraft fire, and there were numerous losses in take-off and landing accidents as a result of mechanical failure. Aside from aircraft destroyed, it should be noted that the Luftwaffe suffered an astonishing *total* casualty toll of 6,047 aircrew dead, missing, wounded or captured during the campaign. Whilst the Luftwaffe had participated in the defeat of most of northwest Europe, it had come at a very considerable cost – around 1,887 aircraft were lost (of all types) by the Luftwaffe and around 1,049 fighters by the RAF.

The RAF could field almost 650 frontline fighters at the start of the Battle of Britain. During the subsequent campaign, RAF Fighter Command lost 1,049 aircraft to all causes, with 535 pilots killed or missing and ten captured. However, the aircraft losses were always made good. Although the strength of RAF Fighter Command in terms of available fighters stood at 644 at the start of the Battle of Britain on 10 July 1940, this figure had increased to 708 in August, 746 in September and 734 in October.

Sqn Ldr John Badger was CO of No. 43 Sqn for seven weeks during the Battle of Britain, prior to being mortally injured when he was impaled on the bough of a tree after bailing out of his Hurricane near Woodchurch, Kent, on 30 August 1940. All of his victories were over bombers, and he claimed multiple Ju 87s, Ju 88s, He 111s and Do 17s during his brief spell in the frontline. (Author's Collection)

Leading Bomber Killers During the Battle of Britain

Name	Bomber Victories	Final Score (all types)	Unit(s) in 1940
Sqn Ldr John Badger	10 and 1 sh	10 and 1 sh	No. 43 Sqn
Sgt Herbert Hallowes	9 and 1 sh	17 and 2 sh	No. 43 Sqn
Plt Off Hamilton Upton	8 and 1 sh	10 and 1 sh	No. 43 Sqn
Plt Off John McGrath	7	18	No. 601 Sqn
Flt Lt Michael Crossley	6 and 1 sh	20 and 2 sh	No. 32 Sqn
Flt Lt Archibald McKellar	6 and 1 sh	17 and 3 sh	No. 605 Sqn
Sqn Ldr Douglas Bader	6	20 and 4 sh	Nos. 222 and 242 Sqns
Sgt Basil Whall	5 and 2 sh	7 and 2 sh	Nos. 263 and 602 Sqns
Sqn Ldr Robert Tuck	5 and 1 sh	27 and 2 sh	Nos. 92 and 257 Sqns
Plt Off Frank Carey	5	25 and 3 sh	Nos. 3 and 43 Sqns
Sgt Josef Frantisek	5	17	No. 303 Sqn
Sgt James Lacey	5	28	No. 501 Sqn
Plt Off Eric Lock	5	26	No. 41 Sqn

OPPOSITE

Gun cameras were fitted in some RAF fighters during the Battle of Britain and operated when the 0.303-in. weapons were fired. By this method, cine film could be used to assess accuracy and results. This camera is fitted in a Hurricane of No. 501 Sqn. (Author's Collection)

AFTERMATH

Although air fighting over Britain continued way beyond the 'official' end of the Battle of Britain on 31 October 1940, the instances where RAF fighters encountered Luftwaffe bombers over the British Isles were becoming few and far between. Aside from a brief incursion by fighter-escorted Italian bombers over the east coast on 11 November 1940, escorted Luftwaffe bomber formations had disappeared from British skies by mid-October 1940, and the large fighter-versus-bomber engagements that had been typical of the summer of 1940 just petered out.

After mid-October, the Luftwaffe restricted its mass-bombing offensive almost exclusively to the hours of darkness, and bombers only appeared over the mainland singly whilst engaged on either nuisance raids or armed reconnaissance sorties. On a few occasions, these lone aircraft encountered either patrolling or scrambled RAF fighters and, for the most part, they paid the price. Nuisance raids continued through late 1940 and into 1941, and beyond that for much of the remainder of the war with, for instance, Do 217s conducting solitary daylight nuisance raids well into 1942, along with the 'tip-and-run' raids by Bf 109 and Fw 190 *Jabo* fighter-bombers.

Whilst it cannot be said that the Battle of Britain was an outright victory for RAF Fighter Command in that it had not irrevocably and conclusively 'defeated' the Luftwaffe *per se*, it had, nonetheless, prevented the Luftwaffe from achieving air superiority. By doing so, it had stopped the *Kampfgeschwaderen* from undertaking mass attacks, even with considerable fighter escort, on targets in Britain during the hours of daylight. This alone was no mean achievement, and as bomber losses rose, so the Luftwaffe high command tied the fighter escorts ever more closely to their charges. Such a tactic, born out of desperation, did not work, and with an attrition rate that was becoming intolerable, and the very life blood of the Luftwaffe bomber force draining away on British soil or in the English Channel, the tactics had to be changed.

In doing so, the Luftwaffe exploited the RAF's then woefully inadequate nightfighter defences and the largely ineffective anti-aircraft batteries by simply using the cover of darkness. In this way, the Luftwaffe bomber force pretty much avoided contact with RAF fighters, save for the then relatively unlikely event of an encounter with a nightfighter. Additionally, this change of tactic was a reprieve for RAF Fighter Command and Britain's defence infrastructure,

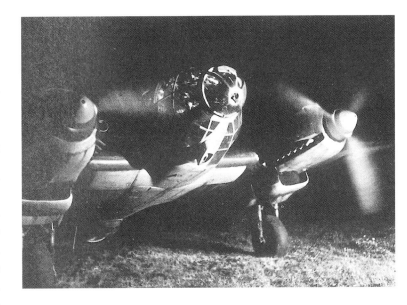

With daylight losses becoming prohibitive, the Luftwaffe increasingly made use of the cover of darkness when it came to attacking targets over Britain in the final months of 1940. (Tony Holmes Collection)

which no longer took the brunt of the attacks. Instead, carpet bombing of industrial, commercial and residential districts took the place of raids aimed primarily at military and RAF assets.

Whilst a great deal had been learned by RAF Fighter Command in relation to the best methods for dealing with escorted and unescorted bomber formations, and even in the specifics of attacking individual bombers, such formations would not be encountered again, in daylight, over the British Isles. Similarly, the Luftwaffe had learned the dangers and realised that even an escorted bomber force was likely to pay a heavy penalty when confronted with determined fighter opposition. Additionally, it had learned that unescorted bomber formations, or singletons, could not simply rely on defensive fire to provide adequate protection. It was a lesson that most air forces of World War II ended up learning the hard way.

At the end of the Battle of Britain, an analysis was undertaken by the Air Ministry of RAF day fighter defensive operations during the 54-day period from 8 August to 30 September, inclusive – the most intensive and critical part of the battle for Fighter Command. The average strength of Fighter Command over this period was 50 squadrons, which was equivalent to a force of about 600 aircraft. They flew a total of 34,967 operational sorties, of which 69 per cent were 'scrambles' with orders to intercept enemy aircraft, 21 per cent were sector patrols, seven per cent were for convoy and shipping protection, and three per cent were for miscellaneous patrols. The maximum effort attained was 1,320 sorties in one day, with more than 1,000 sorties per day being achieved on four separate occasions. The daily average for the whole period of 54 days was just under 650 sorties.

An average of only 23 per cent of the total operational sorties, however, actually engaged the enemy. Eliminating convoy patrols and other sorties that were not normally expected to have an engagement and taking into account only those squadrons ordered to intercept, this figure rises to just 31 per cent. This is indicative of the *relative* crudeness and inefficiency of the command and control system at that time. If just the fighter sorties that engaged the enemy are considered, the battle

From early October 1940 onwards, bomber units started to tone down the camouflage and markings of their aircraft as they embraced nocturnal missions with the ramping up of the night 'Blitz'. This trio of Ju 88As from 9./KG 51 have both painted out and full colour national insignia. (Tony Holmes Collection)

casualty wastage figure over the whole period of 54 days is one fighter lost per 6.5 sorties engaging the enemy.

In the Battle of Britain, the area subject to attack and the disposition and relative strength of the opposing forces placed the RAF at a serious tactical disadvantage. As a result of this, for the greater part of the period under consideration for this analysis, defensive fighters were largely deployed as separate squadrons, thereby adding to inefficiencies of the command and control system. The tactical advantage enjoyed by the Luftwaffe also necessitated a considerable precautionary patrol effort by RAF Fighter Command.

For now, though, the Battle of Britain had been 'won'. The battered and weary bomber force along the Channel coast was withdrawn as the Germans looked eastwards to the Soviet Union. However, whilst the initial stages of Operation *Barbarossa* – launched in June 1941 – were a success thanks to air superiority being quickly established over the Soviet air force, the battles in the West and the Balkans had inflicted losses the Luftwaffe had not fully made good. By the conclusion of the Balkans campaign, the strain put on German resources and the effect on production was already showing. The Luftwaffe had only 1,511 bombers available for operations on 21 June 1941, compared with 1,711 on 10 May 1940. Losses of materiel were simply not being made up. On the other hand, production of British fighters allowed RAF Fighter Command to keep its head above water, despite mostly falling below anticipated output during 1940.

Overall, the Luftwaffe had remained much the same size, but it was weaker in crew quality than it had been in 1939 owing to the losses it had suffered, even in the successful campaigns. The failures in production would lead to the Luftwaffe being severely depleted by the end of the year. However, the planning for *Barbarossa* went ahead, regardless of those failures and issues, and in the face of experience in Western Europe which had shown that reserves needed to be created to replace losses.

In a document produced by the Luftwaffe General Staff on 15 November 1940, it was clear that production was barely adequate to maintain current strengths and frontline units were barely holding their own in terms of personnel establishment. And that was without countenancing any expansion of the Luftwaffe or widening its strategic aims. The document stated that 'Germany's own aircraft production at best ensures maintenance of the present strength. Expansion is impossible, either in personnel or in material.'

The efforts of RAF Fighter Command during the Battle of France and then the Battle of Britain had taken a heavy and unexpected toll on the Luftwaffe bomber force. So much so, in fact, that operations against the Soviet Union were seriously compromised or impaired because of it.

FURTHER READING

BOOKS

Air Historical Branch, *The Battle of Britain – RAF Narrative* (A.H.B., circa 1949)

Beedle, Jimmy, *The Fighting Cocks – 43 (Fighter) Squadron* (Pen & Sword, 2011)

Collier, Basil, *The Defence of The United Kingdom* (HMSO, 1957)

Collier, Richard, *Eagle Day* (Hodder & Stoughton, 1966)

Crook, D. M., *Spitfire Pilot* (Faber, 1941)

Dierich, Wolfgang, *Kampfgeschwader 'Greif'* (Motor Buch Verlag, 1975)

Eimannsberger, Ludwig von, *Zerstorer Gruppe* (Schiffer, 1998)

Foreman, John, *RAF Fighter Command Victory Claims* (Red Kite, 2003)

Goss, Chris, *Brothers in Arms* (Crecy, 1994)

Goss, Chris, *Luftwaffe Bombers' Battle of Britain* (Crecy, 2000)

Goss, Chris, *Luftwaffe Bombers in The Blitz* (Crecy, 2000)

Green, William, *Warplanes of The Third Reich* (Doubleday, 1973)

Hall, Steve and Quinlan, Lionel, *KG 55 in Focus* (Red Kite, 2000)

Johnstone, Air Vice Marshal 'Sandy', CB, DFC, *Enemy in the Sky* (William Kimber, 1976)

Kent, Gp Capt J. A., *One of The Few* (William Kimber, 1971)

Mason, Francis K., *Battle Over Britain* (McWhirter Twins, 1969)

Mason, Francis K., *The Hawker Hurricane* (Crecy, 2001)

Parker, Nigel, *Luftwaffe Crash Archive* (Red Kite, 2013)

Parry, Simon, *Battle of Britain Combat Archive* (Red Kite, 2018)

Price, Alfred, *The Hardest Day* (Macdonald & Jane's, 1979)

Ramsey, Winston, *The Battle of Britain, Then & Now* (After the Battle, 1980)

Ramsey, Winston, *The Battle of France, Then & Now* (After the Battle, 2007)

Saunders, Andy, *Osprey Aviation Elite Units 9 – No 43 Squadron Cocks* (Osprey Publishing, 2004)

Saunders, Andy, *Battle of Britain RAF Operations Manual* (Haynes, 2015)

Shores, Christopher with Williams, Clive, *Aces High* (Grub Street, 1994)

Weal, John, *Osprey Combat Aircraft 1 – Junkers 87 Stukageschwader 1937–41* (Osprey Publishing, 1997)

Wood, Derek, and Dempster, Derek, *The Narrow Margin* (Hutchinson & Co., 1961)

MAGAZINES

Saunders, Andy, *Battle of Britain: A Nation's Finest Hour* (Time Life, 2016)

Shafer, Robin and Saunders, Andy, *Iron Cross Magazine, Issue 1* (Warners, 2019)

INDEX